TOTNES & BRIDGETOWN RACES

by Peter Wakeham

A Limited Edition
Published by Totnes & Bridgetown Races Company Ltd

225/500

ISBN   9781898964889

Printed by Hedgerow Print
Crediton, Devon EX17 1ES

CONTENTS

Dick Francis and Peter Wakeham, Newton Abbot Races, 1995

FOREWORD

I have known Peter Wakeham for more than half a century, since I was a jockey, and I have always been impressed by his devotion to West Country racing. I first rode in that part of the world in 1948 when I was jockey to the late George Owen, bringing horses to Buckfastleigh and Newton Abbot as well as to the Devon & Exeter racecourse on Haldon Hill for the early August meetings. Such fixtures soon became an integral part of my life and I have now been a regular at Newton Abbot and Exeter races for more than sixty years and I still miss visiting the easy-going track at Buckfastleigh.

In this book, Peter has lovingly brought back to life some of the races and characters from the past and has rekindled in me a passion for racing in Devon.

Dick Francis 2009

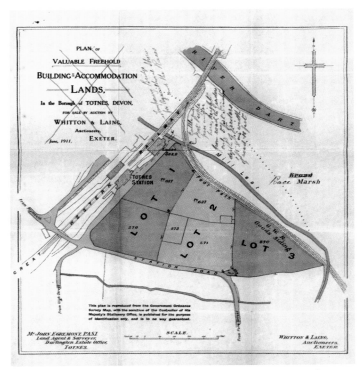

Borough Park, Totnes, in 1911 before development, showing access to the racecourse

THE AUTHOR

The Author has been a Director of Totnes and Bridgetown Races Company since his appointment to the Board in 1983, becoming Chairman in 2008.

He has been involved in West Country point-to-point racing since 1955, when as an owner/trainer he saddled his first runner with an initial winner being recorded the following year. Many successes were to follow in the ensuing twenty-five years with horses from the stable.

Under the same code, he served as the Secretary of the Joint Dart Vale and Haldon and South Pool meetings at Buckfastleigh (1964 – 1977) during which time he became a racecourse commentator, a role that he was to occupy for a period of 34 years. He acted as a local Jockey Club Course Inspector and was for a quarter of a century a Licensed Racecourse Steward under Jockey Club Rules.

Before becoming Chairman of the Devon and Cornwall Point-to-Point Association (1991 – 2003) he was its Programme Editor and represented the area at the P.P.S.A. meetings at Portman Square.

In 2003 he was presented with the Jim Mahon National Award for services to the sport; also the Michael Ayres Award by the South West Racing Club for his contributions to the well-being of Point-to-Point and National Hunt Racing.

ACKNOWLEDGEMENTS

I am grateful for the assistance and encouragement which I have received from my fellow Directors of the Races Company in the compilation of this book, without whose support it would not have materialised: to Mr Roger Michelmore for his visits to Totnes Museum on my behalf; to Mr Robert Savery for collecting and reproducing the photographs; to Mr Anthony Mildmay-White for the loan of the Mildmay Photograph Albums and to Mrs Mary Trueman for supplying a number of Racing Calendars.

I am indebted to Mr Vincent Duggleby, M.B.E., and his wife, Elizabeth (née Frost), who have undertaken much of the legwork involved; for their research, artwork and journalistic advice in this publication. My thanks are also due to them for photographing the Agatha Christie Totnes Races Cup at Greenway House, Brixham, by kind permission of The National Trust.

I thank Mr Alan Langmaid, Administrator of Totnes Museum, for his co-operation in making available press reports from the relevant years and his photocopying service; also to Mr Barrington Weekes of the Totnes Image Bank and Rural Archive, the source of many of the photographs used.

Finally, I am delighted that Mr Dick Francis, C.B.E, has kindly consented to contribute the foreword for this book and thank his son, Mr Felix Francis, for permitting the use of the photograph which appears as a frontispiece.

Peter Wakeham. Rattery. November 2009.

INTRODUCTION

As a child, I recall many tales of the Totnes and Bridgetown Races being recounted by family members, my chief informant being my grandfather, John Wakeham, who for a number of years acted as starter and auctioneer on the course, in addition to having the occasional runner in a race. Sadly, there is no trace of a family success, the best result recorded being a second placing.

In May 1981, the following article appeared in the *Totnes Times* newspaper:

Totnes Racecourse lives again, at least in memory. A race card dated Thursday, September 3rd, 1878 has come to light following an article in the "Times" about the Racecourse and its heyday. It is owned by a Kingsbridge man with memories of visiting the course in 1913 with his father and it is just the sort of reminiscence that two Totnes men were hoping for. Directors of the Totnes and Bridgetown Races Company, Mr Joseph Kellock and Mr 'Togo' Brook, who plan to compile a complete history of the annual racing event, are searching for material, photographs and memories, especially pre-1913. Mr Brook joined the Company as its surveyor and later became its Secretary. He retired as Secretary in 1977 after forty-five years with the Company and was given a seat on the Board of Directors in 1978 to mark this service. Mr Kellock, who was elected to the Board in 1932 in place of the late Charles Barran, became Chairman in 1958 and still serves in that office.

At the time, this request attracted only a limited response but nevertheless resulted in certain additional items of memorabilia being acquired by the Company for their archives. However, the prospective book featuring the history of the races did not materialise, until a small booklet written by Urban Earle and published by the Totnes Community Archive, appeared in 1985. Now, following an interval of nearly thirty years from the original intention, I have, with the co-operation of my fellow Directors of the Company, attempted to record a more in-depth and comprehensive study of the history, events and personalities of this much respected and immensely popular racecourse, together with photographs some of which mirror the action from one hundred years ago.

The exercise of researching and compiling this book has been both fascinating and informative and has given me a better insight into the vision and enterprise of a group of men, who provided the inspiration to construct, maintain and enhance a racecourse at Totnes for the enjoyment of the tens of thousands of spectators, who made their way to Broadmarsh, especially in its early days before the formation of the Company.

I hope that in this book, something may be found to satisfy both the purist and the occasional racegoer who, like our ancestors down through the centuries, enjoyed a day at the races. Where relevant and appropriate, extracts from the press reports of the time have been reproduced as they were written, in their original form, both descriptive and graphic. Maybe this book will revive a few memories for the ever decreasing number of persons who are able to claim that they too were present, over seventy years ago, at the two-day spectacle known as Totnes and Bridgetown Races.

Totnes Annual Diversions 1801.

Fac-simile copy of Totnes Race Programme, 1801, now in possession of Mr. E. Shinner, Stitchford Farm. Printed at the Times Office, Totnes, by request and sold at 6d. each. The proceeds arising from same Mr. Shinner proposes handing over to the Totnes and Ashburton Cottage Hospitals.

Owners of Horfes.	Defcription of Horfes	Names of Horfes.	Horfes Ages.	Meafure of Horfes.		Weights to be carried.		Names of the Riders.	Colours of the Riders Dreffes
				Hds.—In.		St.—lb.			
HUNTERS.									
Mr. Bickford,	Bay Nag,	Bristol,	Aged,	13	3	8	7	Grills,	White,
Mr. Tucker,	Bay Horse,	Win-if-he-can,	5,	13	3½	7	10½	Conybeare,	
Mr. Chapple,	Bay Nag,	Cottager,	Aged,	14	1	9	7	Lang,	
Mr. Chapple,	Bay Horse,	Borrington,	Aged,	14	1½	9	10½	Guy,	Yellow and Black,
GALLOWAYS.									
Mr. Fitzgeralds,	Bay Mare,	Betsey,	Aged,	13	3½	8	10½	Guy,	Yellow and Black,
Mr. Predum	Chesnut Horse	Rock,	6,	13	2½	7	10½	Barrel,	Blue
Mr. White	Bay Mare,	Camilla,	4,	13	2	6	7	Stockman,	Yellow and White,
Mr. Harvey,	Chesnut Nag,	Infant,	3,	13	3	6	7		
PONIES.									
Mr. Davis,	Bay Nag,	Little John,	6,	12	3			Boon,	Green and White,
Mr. Gofs,	Black Nag,	Danceaway,		13				John Gilpin,	Yellow,
Mr. Williams,	Black Mare,			13					
Mr. Parford,	Gray Nag,	Poor Tom,	Aged,	12	1				

[PRICE ONE PENNY.]

C. FISHER, Printer and Stationer, TOTNES.

Totnes Races programme 1801

4

CHAPTER 1
TOTNES AND BRIDGETOWN

Totnes is an ancient municipal borough and market town, picturesquely situated on the western bank of the River Dart whilst on the opposite bank is Bridgetown, which at one time was part of the parish of Berry Pomeroy. The town is served by a station on the main Paddington to Penzance railway, which at the time of the Totnes and Bridgetown Races was operated by the Great Western Railway. The town is to be found approximately midway between Exeter and Plymouth being twenty-three miles in distance from the former and twenty-four miles from the latter, whilst Torquay is some nine miles distant with other principal towns such as Kingsbridge twelve miles, Dartmouth ten miles and Newton Abbot ten miles, being well known centres of population.

Totnes is situated in an area of Devon known as the South Hams which is often referred to as the 'Garden of Devon' and abounds in rolling hills and rich pasture. The town is connected to Bridgetown by a stone bridge built in 1828 which was a toll bridge until 1881. A further bridge known as the Brutus Bridge was later constructed in 1982 to permit through traffic to avoid the town centre, spanning the River Dart at the southern end of the racecourse. Downstream is to be found Vire Island, a small island in the river, planted with trees and shrubs, which is used for walks and recreational purposes by the public. The River Dart which is navigable and flows to Dartmouth provided an arterial and important link to the town and racecourse by means of passenger steamer and barge, the latter form of conveyance being essential to the timber, coal and sand industries which used to flourish along the quayside. The river is tidal up to the weir and as we shall discover in a later chapter, this presented its own problems for racing prior to 1914. Totnes was also endowed with a cottage hospital, conveniently situated on Bridgetown hill less than a mile from the course and which, since its erection in 1901, provided a necessary service to the races for the benefit of spectator and jockey alike.

During the 19th century and prior to World War II, an abundant number of hostelries and inns were to be found in the town, all of which became extremely well patronized during the race week. Familiar establishments to be found included The Bell Inn, The Dartmouth Inn, The Globe Hotel, and The King William IV - whose landlord Tommy Newcombe was a well known character on the racecourse and in his later years rang the mounting bell for jockeys at Buckfastleigh Races. Other licensed premises were the Kingsbridge Inn, the Lord Nelson, the Oxford Arms, the Plymouth Inn, the Waterman's Arms, the Royal Seven Stars Hotel and the Seymour Hotel at Bridgetown, the latter two providing the more superior accommodation for overnight guests.

Totnes through the centuries has been the centre of a number of sporting activities, hunting being the premier pastime for its country folk. Served by two packs of hounds, the South Devon Foxhounds and the Dart Vale Harriers (formerly the Berry Harriers), both packs held meets in and around the town. Popular venues included the Seymour Hotel during the 1950s and later it was the scene for the Dart Vale and Haldon Harriers' opening meet, whilst the traditional Boxing Day meet was held on The Plains, both of these events being well supported. The Rotherfold, Bowden Pillars, Bourton Hall (in later years renamed the Chateau Bellevue Hotel) and Weston Tree were other favoured meeting places in the area.

Totnes & District Agricultural Show has been in existence since 1918 and between the wars was situated on the racecourse at Broadmarsh before moving to its two present sites at Berry Pomeroy following its post-war resumption. Horse shows and gymkhanas were popular features in the town during the 1950s, taking place in the Borough Park which backs on to the racecourse. Additional features at these events often included a rodeo in which unbroken ponies from Dartmoor, and on one occasion steers, were the mounts which challenged both the experienced and foolhardy alike, as they attempted to stay on board.

Point-to-point racing (the amateur version of steeplechasing for horses which had been qualified by hunting with a pack of hounds) took place at Gerston Farm from 1957 to 1962, before returning again to the area when a course was established at Bowden Pillars in 1979, just a stone's throw from Gerston. Both of these fixtures were promoted by the Dart Vale and Haldon Harriers.

A cattle market was situated at the top of the town adjacent to the Rotherfold. Special bull sales and sheep auctions were held on the Borough Park which were patronized by local farmers. Owing to the cramped conditions under which the market operated, it was transferred during the early 1960s to a site at Broadmarsh on the old Racecourse (now an industrial estate), being purpose-built and opened by Her Majesty Queen Elizabeth II. After an enthusiastic beginning, the enterprise was slow to get off the ground and become established. It struggled on for a few years but never enjoyed the support or popularity of its counterparts at Newton Abbot and Exeter, before its closure and redevelopment.

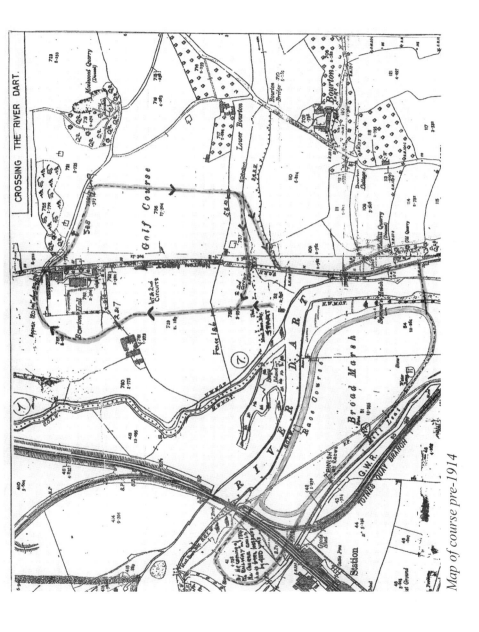

Map of course pre-1914

1900. Mr H Bulteel's Euphrasia (3rd) followed by Mr H G Hawker's Sailaway crossing the River Dart

Runners crossing the River Dart on the homeward journey circa 1902

Racing on the Bourton Marsh, circa 1906

Spectators view runners crossing the River Dart, circa 1906. Redhill Quarry in background

On the way to the 3 mile start accompanied by the Clerk of the Course circa 1903

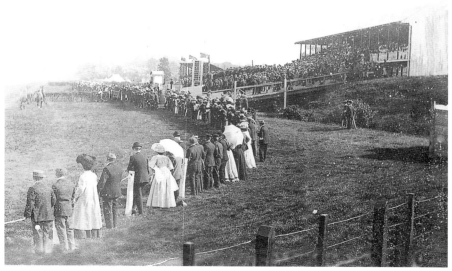

Crowds lining the bend after the winning post. Note the packed grandstands and footbridge access over the leat. Early 20th century
Photo courtesy of Totnes Image Bank & Rural Archive

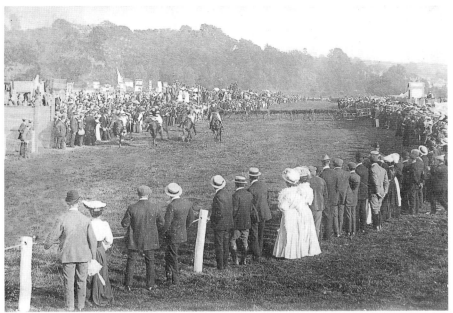

View of finishing straight with three horses passing winning post, Judges'
box and number board on right. Early 20th century
Photo courtesy of Totnes Image Bank & Rural Archive

Mr F B Mildmay, M.P., a Steward at the meeting and Mrs Mildmay circa 1910
Photo courtesy of Totnes Image Bank & Rural Archive

View from grandstand over the leat to the Paddock, offices and bookmakers circa 1910
Photo courtesy of Totnes Image Bank & Rural Archive

CHAPTER 2
EARLY DAYS

It is not possible to pinpoint with accuracy the exact year when racing commenced at Totnes but it is almost certain to have been in the mid 1780s. This is based on three press reports, two of which appeared in the *Totnes Times*. The first of these concerned a local lady who had informed the newspaper in 1861 that her mother had told her that she had been born the year that racing began in 1785. This may not appear at first appraisal to be of great significance bearing in mind the vagaries of the human mind but nevertheless events which are linked with family dates of birth, marriage and death cannot easily be dismissed. The second piece of evidence is contained in a letter written to the newspaper in 1898 and entitled "The Origin of Totnes Races", signed T.H. which I reproduce in its entirety:

"Sir,

I have so recently joined a gentleman of sporting fame of the Veterinary Infirmary, Union Street, Plymouth, in a correspondence of sporting matters in Totnes and as his last letter contains matters of so much importance to the sporting world, I think they should have the benefit of it.

In the first place I learn that Totnes Races owed their origin to sporting events that took place at Malborough, near Kingsbridge, in 1786 under the name of "The Kingsbridge Diversions", after three years transferred to East Allington and finally to Totnes in 1791. It was then that the great-grandfather of Mr Richard Heath was appointed the first Clerk of the Course, a position worthily filled by the Heath family for more than a hundred years. It was in the early years 1800-30 that Totnes gained much fame for the 'honour' of racing when gold and silver cups of rare value from £50 to £100 were exhibited in the shop window of Louis Jacobs, Jeweller, in the house now occupied by Mrs Tabor. My correspondent regrets that real sporting tastes have given place to a more rapid period when money seems to be the 'be all'.

We have, however, seen steeplechases at Totnes that would do honour to the sporting world since 1846, when steeplechases were first introduced here and without flattery I may state that in Harry Deacon we have seen the boldest and most accomplished gentleman rider that had ever ridden on any course. Many years since, I took the trouble to walk to Mock Wood at Pheasant's Hill to see the extraordinary leaps that Deacon used to take on Edgar. Coming down at a rapid rate over the steep field by Mock Wood, he used to take a flying leap over a deep and dangerous lane, with a high hedge on either side into the field below; and woe betide others that attempted the same terrific breakneck course, for immediately on emerging from this terrible leap, a high hedge had to be cleared. It was here that a splendid horse called Vengeance fell and, breaking its back, had to be destroyed. Mr Deacon deserved well of the racing world for he brought to Totnes such celebrities as Challenger, Little Monkey and The Fawn, besides old favourites Edgar, Egbert and Mohawk; and the bold rider disregarded a broken arm, riding at one time with his arm in a sling and winning one of his six, £50.00 triumphs in succession on beautiful Edgar. If I mistake not, Deacon won an exciting race with Challenger, in one of our earliest steeplechases in 1849.

It has been refreshing to me to hear our Plymouth friend speak highly of races in former years, when Tom Carlyle owned the noted horse, Allow Me, which with a celebrated racer called Wortham, ran two successive dead heats for the Tradesman's Plate, the Committee dividing the stakes as the two horses could not be separated.

To show the value of horseracing, this Plymouth friend owned a young Allow Me, the very best that man ever crossed, and on it its owner in five weeks saw nine foxes killed on Dartmoor. He speaks also of other races in which Little Charley (Bond) won the Grand South Hams in 1862 and afterwards was ridden in the hunting field. As a reason for Galloway racing in heats horses above 13 hands paid a tax of £2-12s-0d a year; under 13 hands, £1 (but our friend is not exactly right here, for thoroughbred horses had also to run heats – for instance Sir John Buller's Why Not). The sporting community will be glad to learn that our champion, Mr Deacon, is perfectly well and hearty in Hampshire where, a few years since, he was Master of the H.H. (Hampshire Hunt) hounds. I believe in answer to the enquiry into the match for £50 between Mr E Bond's Metal and Mr Deer's Betty-go-by-'em the race was not run at a regular race meeting but on an afternoon set apart for the purpose in September 1858, when Deer's horse bolted at the Railway Arch and ran into mud, Metal winning easily."

The third contribution for consideration as to the origin of Totnes Races is by way of an article which came to light in a publication entitled *Kingsbridge and Salcombe* and was handed to me by a fellow Director of the Company, Mr Robert Savery of South Brent. It is an extract from a chapter describing the wreck of the Ramillies in 1760 near the cove and village of Inner Hope, the road to which from Kingsbridge is through Malborough and six miles distant.

The open down or common called The Bolt belonging to Lord Viscount Courtenay adjoins this point of land. Here the neighbouring gentry established races on 29th day of May 1768, or as they were then denominated, "The Kingsbridge Annual Diversions", and ponies and Galloways contended for prizes of less than fifty pounds, while various other competitions for propounded reward crowned the day. They were held here every year in the month of June till 1771 when they were removed to a better course on the Middle "Sewer" (sic.) – probably Soar – in the same parish, where they continued each summer till the farmer converted the grounds to tillage in 1782 and then these amusements were changed to Wallaton Downs in the parish of East Allington, where they expired that year. From the ashes of these sprang the Totnes Races which commenced the subsequent season (1784) and are still continued.

So there we have it, three marginally different conclusions as to the precise year. To summarise, the lady whose mother was born in the same year of 1785, the lengthy letter to the Editor of the *Totnes Times* whose writer plumped for 1791 and the report on the sinking of the Ramilies which opted for 1784. The two latter publications both referred to the Malborough and East Allington connection which confirms the credibility of those reports.

The Totnes course was sited at Broadmarsh, a plain bordering the River Dart lying on its western bank adjacent to the town and railway line from Newton Abbot with its station no more than half a mile distant. It was a predominately flat, right-handed track of approximately six furlongs, with the finishing straight and grandstand backing on to Borough Park. After the winning post came an acute bend before runners set out on the next circuit. The outstanding feature prior to 1913 was the double crossing of the River Dart in the long distance races. Before the advent of the railway in 1847 the course followed the line of the track right up to the weir below Bourton Hall (later to become the Chateau Bellevue Hotel) before crossing the Newton Abbot to Totnes main road and climbing the hill, then swinging right handed around Mock Wood passing out of sight from the grandstand, before reappearing around the quarry and descending Pheasant's Hill to the road over which the horses raced for nearly half a mile. Re-crossing the river by the Ropeworks where the main road flattens before entering Bridgetown, the runners proceeded up the short straight to the winning post. The river crossings were concreted in an effort to fill all potholes and to produce a sound surface but as the river was tidal the course was subject to flooding at high tide, making perfect timing for the meeting essential. On at least one occasion it was recorded that poor timing was responsible for both horses and jockeys having to swim for it. A scribe whose pen name was 'Idler' suggested in the *Totnes Times* that the purpose of the road section was to drive home the nails in the horses' shoes which had been loosened by the holding nature of the ground. Undoubtedly the writer was alluding to the fact that the course on the Bourton side of the river did not always follow the same layout each year as variations had to be made to accommodate farming practices. This distinctive layout also gave rise to allegations of malpractice from time to time with riders suspected of giving their mounts prolonged breathers under the archway which carried the Buckfastleigh, Staverton and Ashburton branch railway and again behind the quarry and wood above the road.

Prior to the formation of the Company in 1928, a consortium of local men were responsible for the promotion of the races and leased the land at

Broadmarsh from the Duke of Somerset whilst negotiations with farmers on the other side of the river did not always run smoothly and became the cause of some friction. The leased area was subsequently purchased from the Duke by the Company.

In the early days the course had been entirely of banks but soon became interspersed with flat races, hurdle races and "over the flying course" which referred to a combination of birch fences, flights of hurdles and a stone wall. A description of the banking course in 1898 is contained in the Totnes Times report of that year.

"The race was run over the very trying banking course around the quarries. Magpie was first away with Caprice lying next and Commander third, about six lengths dividing the trio as they raced past the stand. Before going into the country, the horses had to go twice over the fences on the marsh itself and the same order was maintained, all playing a waiting game. The river was safely forded and then Caprice took up the running, the favourite (Magpie) dashed ahead, but then went the wrong side of a flag and Caprice went away with the race well in hand. Commander refused the bank by Bourton Hall, but got over at the second attempt, only to refuse the next obstacle. Meanwhile the favourite drew up in the turnip field, but at the bank at the bottom, came a cropper and threw Gregor, who was however unhurt and Caprice walked home a worthy winner. Magpie came in sometime after and Commander did not complete the course. Even if he had done so, he could not have taken any prize as he failed to jump the water dyke at the bottom of the course, just after the start."

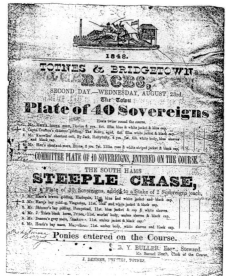

An early racecard 1848

CHAPTER 3
A CENTURY'S RACING (1800 – 1900)

The official Racing Calendar of 1800 provides the first detailed record of racing at Totnes. A meeting held in 1799 is mentioned and we know that racing had been in existence since the mid 1780s but that these meetings were intermittent and were not held every year. Gaps would occur before the action would resume. Each year a two-day fixture was advertised which took place during the first fortnight in September but there were exceptions, e.g. in 1848 when 22nd and 23rd August were favoured. The principal races in 1800 were run in heats of three miles with weights to be carried of between twelve and thirteen stones. There were also races for Galloways, ponies and hacks who competed for minor prizes compared to their more illustrious companions. Between 1820 and 1836 there were races for a gold cup with a nominal value of £100 and silver cups to the value of £50 each. The Company has in its possession a silver cup dated 1794 which is engraved, "Totnes Races, John Hayles Sheckle, Esq. won by Boringdon, property of M Chappell". This trophy was purchased by the Company from Brufords of Exeter in 1951 and is now valued at over £2,000. In the absence of trophies, races during the nineteenth century carried prize money of between thirty and fifty sovereigns, not inconsiderable sums for the period, as cottages could have been purchased for these amounts at the time.

A newspaper report from 1860 detailed the running of the Totnes Steeplechase for a prize of fifty sovereigns, the gift of His Grace the Duke of Somerset,together with a stake of five sovereigns each runner. This resulted in a win for Mr Holman's Little Monkey ridden by his son in a field of eight. The horses were described as being in "fine" condition and nearly all thoroughbreds. Some amusement was caused when the closely bunched group crossed the river, causing a perfect cloud of spray, the water being rather deep at the time. At the cornfield ascending the hill, Flying Empress refused a fence unseating her rider, taking a circuit through the uncut portion of the corn. Upon coming back onto the road, Cardinal appeared likely to win having a several lengths advantage but after crossing the river fell in some mud. Before he could be restarted the others had passed. The second placed Wrestler finished with his jockey Gregory carrying a stirrup which had broken at the third fence.

There can be no better description of the scene which greeted racegoers than that reported in the *Totnes Times and Dartmoor Gazette* (price one penny) and dated September 12th, 1868.

"Year after year this annual holiday attains notoriety but perhaps never has it passed off under more favourable auspices than the present gathering or most justly deserved the title given it, a few years since, by an eminent sporting contemporary, 'The unrivalled meeting of the West ...' As early as

Monday, Totnes was visited by its usual characters, shooting galleries, shows, standings, etc. The townspeople also willing to meet the demands of their visitors, commenced preparations and at an early period of the week, the hotels, inns and refreshment houses presented quite an attractive appearance... We believe from the way in which our streets were continually flocked by strangers that ample justice must have been done to all ... Good business must have been done by the publicans, for we were much amused by observing in different roads two or three rows of equipages, which consisted of the aristocratic coach and four in hand, down to the costermonger's donkey cart. From whence all the traps came it is impossible to say, but certainly some of the vehicles which 'had seen the light of better days' were brought out once more to swell the numbers. On the course the usual class of persons and amusements which are characteristic of such meetings were present, only a much larger collection than has ever before been recollected. The various shows and exhibitions occupied some very considerable portion of the course and extended in a direct line about a quarter of a mile in length. Large numbers of itinerant musicians and negro troupes were incessantly striking up all sorts of negro ditties. Punch and Judy were also there and added greatly to the amusement of the large concourse of people, as there were also large numbers forming a half circle around the model house. Aunt Sallies gaudily arrayed were on the ground but failed to attract much attention; and the thimble riggers and card sharps, being pretty closely looked after by the 'Bobbies' did not transact quite so much business as they could have wished. The sellers of Brummagen jewellery were exceedingly active but the number of "flats" are gradually declining, having paid for learning on previous occasions. The course was in capital condition for the racing and excellent order was preserved during the time of the racing, several members of the County Constabulary having been specially engaged by the Committee for that purpose. The two stands erected by Mr S Reeves deserve special comment. They were each 144 feet in length, which is about half as long again as those of some ten or a dozen years ago; but only twelve feet longer than those of last year (which is a striking proof that the races are gradually improving) and built in a most complete and substantial manner, and they were, we are pleased to state, well filled... They contained a large number of the elite of the neighbourhood and also from all parts of the country. The fair sex, who were gaily attired in all the fashions of the season, added much to the brilliancy of the scene and caused the stands to present a most charming appearance. The first class Band of the South Devon Militia under Mr S Fly attended on both days.

There was an innovation on the first day in the matter of cards and lists of the running horses, the printer on the first day (Mr Denner) declining to issue any penny lists, in consequence of some of the sellers last year of adopting the ingenious plan of pasting penny lists on old cards and pieces of bonnet board and selling them for sixpence. We don't like any innovation calculated to interfere with the popularity of the races and the general public are accustomed to look out at early morning for their penny lists which are convenient also for sending away by post to friends at a distance after the races are over. There is no reason why cards cannot be sold at 3d and lists at 1d. The card for the first day embraced five events, the entries being good; but unfortunately the race for the Yeomanry Steeplechase Plate of twenty sovereigns,for which seven were entered did not come off, in consequence of some of the owners objecting to compete with Mr T Shore's Barumite (except on certain terms), as they contended that horse was not of the proper class, being thoroughbred. As Mr Shore would neither accept the terms proposed for sharing, or withdraw his horse, the field was reduced below the requisite number of three, and consequently the race fell through."

A description of the running of the Totnes Steeplechases gives a clear indication of the route taken once the first river crossing had been completed.

"The course was pretty much the same as in former years, the horses crossing the river first under the railway bridge, entering Mr Shinner's Marsh and down by the side of the river until crossing Hempston Lake, when they make for the hill. After taking several hedges they round the quarry and the horses are afterwards lost to view for a short time. (N.B. Owing to rumours of malpractice by some riders when out of sight, the course was altered in later years so that the runners remained visible at all times.) On their reappearance they descended the hill, go through some meadows and enter the Exeter road (so described at the time, but in fact better known as the Totnes-Newton Abbot road) where they proceed as far as Redhill Quarry, then into Mr Barter's Marsh, across the river for the spin up the marsh to the winning post, thereby completing about three and a half miles of hunting country."

In a later contest on the same day, a flat race run over 1½ miles for a plate of fifteen sovereigns, four horses went to post. Even though no obstacles were to be encountered events did not progress at all smoothly. The report on the race states that Gilead went away with the lead with Minnie second, Little Port third and Theory in the rear. The horses ran in capital style and kept their respective positions for a short time when Minnie, evidently a strong self-willed horse, passed Gilead and bolted from the course and took a flying leap over the wall, thereby throwing the rider Hayes. The horse then rushed among the mass of people and after being driven into the mill leat was soon captured. The popularity and amazing scenes to have been witnessed in 1868 (this was the assumed two-day fixture at which a total of 50,000 were deemed to have been present) were further reported as a result of the second day's card.

"Yesterday (Thursday) opened with brilliant prospects – the weather being beautifully fine and the sun shining from morning to evening with the full splendour of summer which this year appears loath to come to an end. Visitors from all parts flocked into the ancient town in every imaginable way, by river, by rail and by road, the managers of the railway and steamboat traffic, exerting themselves to their utmost and most successfully to accommodate the public. We should say the railway never contributed so large a quota before; nor was there any falling off in gay equipages, the numbers of four in hand being very large, especially from Plymouth and other western towns. Torquay also contributed a good number of very fashionable vehicles, with good teams. The road to the course by the mill leat from one to two o'clock was the scene of extraordinary bustle – one continuous line of people moving onward to the race-ground. The well stored hampers on the tops of the coaches, buses and brakes, showed that the visitors had come once more to enjoy their annual picnic; and the lines of vehicles by the roadside near the different hostelries was a sign that must be seen to be believed – showing altogether that the mass of people throughout South Devon regard Totnes Races as their best holiday for the year. We do not profess to be an unerring judge of the numbers congregated in so heterogeneous a mass of people but it was the universal remark that no one had ever seen a larger number present than on this occasion."

Several horses which had run on the previous day turned out again (not an unusual occurrence). However Barumite, who was the cause of the abandonment of the Yeomanry Steeplechase on the first day, turned up as fresh as paint the next day contesting the Grand South Hams Steeplechase carrying top weight of 12st. 7lb. The race description reports that after a circuit of Broadmarsh Barumite had dropped away as the field crossed the river on the outward journey. Upon reaching the Exeter road the rider put on "a bit of a spurt" closing up, but on climbing the hill became tailed off. The runners continued to the top of the hill and are reported "as passing over the top of Bourton Quarry, the lot were lost to view for a little while, having to go through a copse". Our friend, Barumite drew the comment that "it was believed by some that the reason for his figuring so badly was done in order not to carry extra at the forthcoming meeting at Exeter next week". This, however, was not to be the last that was to be seen of Barumite on the day, for later in the afternoon he turns up again in The Committee Plate of twenty sovereigns a flat race over 1½ miles for which six ran and in which ridden by Mr T Jackson (as opposed to Roberts in the steeplechase) he carried the top weight of 10st., weights for the other participants ranging from 8st. 8lb. down to 8st.

The race was reported as follows: Two horses from the original entry of eight were scratched, the reason given for one being that it was not able to obtain the services of a jockey light enough to do the weight. After one false start, the horses got off. Minnie was the first to leave her companions and on rounding the further corner led by about a length with Barumite second and the remainder well up, all of a heap and going a slashing pace. On reaching the bottom of the course, Minnie exhibited her usual bad temper and left her companions running straight down the marsh towards the river, her rider having no control whatever over her. After this she altered her course and came up the straight at a good speed but when reaching the grandstand she again bolted 'slap bang' among the people and threw Maslen over her head onto the railings. Barumite now had the lead, closely waited on by Little Port, Hercules and Theory being in the rear. These respective positions were kept to the finish, Barumite winning "easily". For owner, Mr T Shore, it was a case of "all's well that ends well".

A description of the final race on the card illuminated other pitfalls which befell runners. This was a 3½ mile handicap steeplechase for which nine ran. One, however, pulled up shortly after starting. After crossing the river several horses refused the fence in Mr Holman's field, leaving only four to continue. Whilst crossing the Exeter road, "the hindermost horses were interrupted by some horsemen coming down the roadway and they consequently refused to take the fence for some time. The horses were thus divided into two batches." Three finished with only a length dividing the winner, Fire Eater, from the runner up, Forest King, with Willow, a bad third.

It will already have been noted that the crowd of 50,000 was for an assumed two-day meeting and every reference that I have seen reported had it so, indeed the *Totnes Times and Dartmouth Gazette* dated September 12th, 1868, only lists the results for the first and second days. However, a closer study reveals that an evening dinner took place after each day's racing which was recorded as follows:

Race Ordinary. In the evening of the first day, the Annual Race Ordinary was held at The Seymour Hotel, when between forty and fifty gentlemen sat down to a sumptuous spread under the Presidency of the Stewards, Maj. Strode S.D.M and V Calmady, Esq. The usual loyal, patriotic and complimentary toasts having been disposed of, the party became convivial and a pleasant evening was spent.

Race Soirées. The annual race soirée came off at The Seymour Hotel on the evening of the second day, when above one hundred ladies and gentlemen attended. The splendid band of the South Devon Militia under the conductorship of Mr Key were in attendance and the proceedings passed off very successfully.

Third Day. There have been the third day's usual winding up races and amusements on the course this (Friday) afternoon and Mr Doel with his accustomed liberality provided a dinner for fifty of the oldest poor persons of Totnes and Bridgetown, each having also a bottle of ale or stout. There were two steeplechases which were closely contested, one won by Gazette and the other by Joe. Mr Barret's Catch-'em-alive won the flat race in two heats. Sport excellent, attendance nearly as large as on the first day.

The total of 50,000 spread over three days would still average a crowd of 16,000 -17,000, a large assembly to be herded onto the small and restricted course. A postscript to the meeting appears in the form of an item which states that "much curiosity was caused on the second day of the races by the exhibition in the shop window of Mr Geo. Penny, fruiterer, Fore Street, Totnes, of some remarkably fine pears of his own growth, one of which weighed twenty-five ounces. The sum of 10 shillings was offered for nine of the largest, but refused, as the handsomest were said to be intended as a present for the Princess Alexandra, after whom the sort has been named.

Some horses created a lasting memory by their exploits. Such a case was Mr Werford's Warbling who in 1828 won the Gold Cup with such ease that the Cup was not competed for again. A candidate for being the best loved horse to have raced on the course was Mr Budge's black mare, Bessie. Described as "honest as steel" she won on the first day in 1874, won two races the following year and also won a match at the only spring meeting in 1876. She unfortunately broke down in the Totnes Flying Steeplechase the same year and died shortly afterwards. She was buried with great solemnity a few days later in a grave positioned near the winning post which had witnessed the scene of her finest hours.

Undoubtedly, the arrival of the railway (1847) made a huge difference to the accessibility and well being of the races not only for the spectator but providing a means of transport for the horses many of which now arrived from relatively distant parts, although the majority of runners were still supplied by local owners and trainers. Boys who previously used to assemble at the Bull Inn waiting for runners to arrive from Plymouth in the hope of earning a few coppers by walking the horses around the Inn's square to cool them down now transferred their attention to the railway yard.

The town of Totnes supported the prize fund, as it is recorded that in 1825 it contributed £34 to the Plate of £50, the remainder being donated by the stewards. This was in respect of what in essence was a Hunter's Steeplechase as the qualification stipulated "for horses that have been regularly hunted in any of the four Western Counties". An interesting fact is that, unlike the present day Hunter Chase, professional jockeys were permitted to compete against the amateur rider in these races.

Despite the great popularity of the fixture not everyone was greatly impressed. The Western Daily Mercury's reporter, "Toller" wrote that, "Enlightenment never comes too late in life but I must admit my old petrified encrusted ideas of steeplechasing received a rude shock before I left". Another scribe stated that no course in the South West is more trying to the stamina of competition than that adopted for steeplechasing at Totnes, this being emphasised by a Maiden Steeplechase which was recorded in 1898, not untypical of the times. The event in question was for four year olds only and run over a distance of 2½ miles and which included the river crossings.

"Pete made the running for the first ¼ mile. Ceres bolted in taking the obstacle near the grandstand and refused another fence a little later on and was out of the running. Pete got across the water first followed by Penarth, Tempest and Reprieve. In going up the hill, Penarth came a cropper in engaging a fence. Gregor (the jockey) was dismounted and did not take further part in the race. Tempest was making the pace when the highest field in the steeplechase was reached. Pete, Reprieve and Redbreast following on ten lengths behind, Reprieve got even with Tempest and both raced down the hill together, Pete and Redbreast shortening the distance between the leaders. Before the run home the horses had to cross the river. Reprieve got there first and got through all right, Tempest took considerable time in doing so and allowed Pete to get into second place. Reprieve was a very popular winner by six lengths from Pete with Tempest a poor third."

Before concluding this chapter I refer to other activities which took place during the race week in and around the town. In the early days bull baiting was held on the third day of the races, at the Rotherfold, the Town Marsh and 'the field on the Ashburton road'. Dogs were imported from Crediton, most showing signs of previous conflict. Their owners and bystanders were often caught up in the melée as they too were tossed as they attempted to break the falls of the dogs whilst women would try to catch them in their aprons. Cock fighting was also the order of the day being advertised on the 1825 race poster, in addition the Gazelle hunt, in which an old ram was thoroughly greased then let loose, the object being for the crowd to catch the animal. I recall from my youth similar events taking place at horse shows and gymkhanas when a pig was substituted for the ram. Other activities in the town included balls, an open air version being a feature in 1861, together with theatre which was the 'Prince of Wales', housed in the Seymour Hotel and "a pretty little thing similar to those of Exeter and Plymouth with its tiers and boxes and galleries". Edmund Keen once played here as did Miss Foote in the role of Little Jockey. During the same week in 1893 Messrs Hybert and Liddle's Dramatic Company staged *Night Mail* to a packed house from which many had to be turned away. The production met with rapturous applause and the receipts amounted to over £50. A fireworks display held at Totnes Castle was an additional attraction in the evening.

It is debatable as to whether the year 1900 should appear as the final year of the nineteenth century or the first of the twentieth century but for the purposes of this book I include it in the former, when the following report appeared in the press:

"Small wonder it is, at every succeeding meeting the 'Derby of the West' as the Totnes fixture is generally called, proved more and more attractive, for the sport is always excellent. Every autumn the attendance at this, the most popular of the Devon fixtures, seems to be larger than it was a year previously and yesterday when the meeting opened, another record attendance must have been created. There was every reason why this should be so apart from the great attractiveness which the Totnes meeting itself possesses for sportsmen in and out of the county, the entries were larger than ever before, the weather was delightfully fine and the warmth of the sun being tempered by a cooling breeze, the nicely situated course and its surroundings were charmingly pretty. The huge crowd which poured into the quaint old Borough and on to the course was rewarded with one of the finest afternoon's racing ever seen at a meeting, the records of which are full of capital sport. With thousands of spectators scattered over it, the course presented an animated scene and the fashionable costumes of the many ladies in the grandstand lent additional colour to the surroundings. There was not a tame race for the day, but the Totnes Hurdle Handicap, the first race on the card, provided one of the finest finishes. With nine starters, it was only in the last hundred yards that Meschina got the better of the second favourite, Sais, by a head and won another victory for Mr J G Bulteel, for whom the filly, at the Plymouth meeting, scored twice. It was, however, regrettable that in this race a disaster should have occurred, which resulted in the death of Ballyshannon, one of the finest animals, which has competed at the Western race meetings and the winner among other events, of the big race at the Three Towns meeting and also that Armstrong, his jockey, should have had his collar bone broken. The horse, after clearing a hurdle in the back straight, broke a blood vessel and after losing his rider, staggered on into the river and was drowned. Despite the number of times Texas has changed hands since the Newton meeting, he is running capitally and pulled off the Bridgetown Selling Steeplechase after a rare tussle with Heron. At the auction owner/rider Mr Longworth lost the horse to Mr G Ryall for the sum of 100 guineas."

Silver cup inscribed 1794, won by M Chappell's Boringdon

Silver cup with tap attachment; dated 1794, won by Thomas Peeke's Sportsman

Aerial view of Totnes, Vire Island below the bridge with the racecourse top right.   Photo courtesy of Totnes Image Bank & Rural Archive

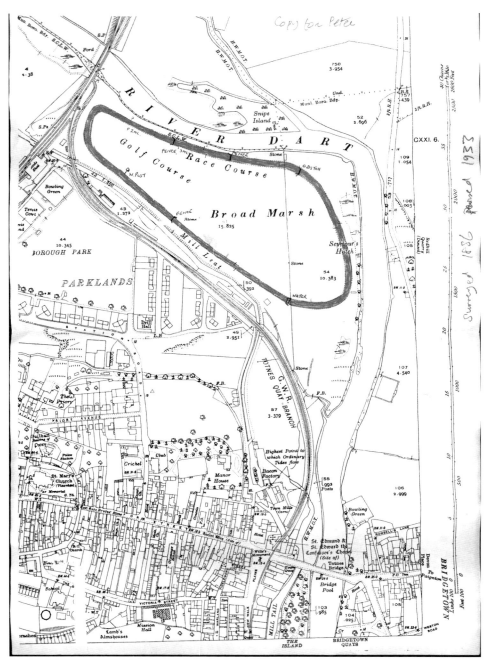

Map of racecourse 1919-38 with racing confined to the West Bank Marshes, showing the grandstands' proximity to the town

1911. Totnes Town Council Fire Engine drawing water from the leat. This engine was used for watering the course. A second appliance can be seen in the background.   *Photo courtesy of Totnes Image Bank & Rural Archive*

The River Dart at high tide illustrating the problems which at times beset the racecourse   *Photo courtesy of Totnes Image Bank & Rural Archive*

Mr John Wakeham, Starter and Auctioneer 1920-38

Horses negotiating the water jump. Note inside track which bypassed the fence on final circuit. Photo courtesy of Totnes Image Bank & Rural Archive

CHAPTER 4
THE PRE-WAR YEARS (1901 – 1914)

At the turn of the century the following little ditty was sung by children in the locality.

Oh, ye young man, take my advice
Beware of painted faces
And mind which way your pony runs
When you're at Totnes races!

Early twentieth century prizemoney showed an increase, now ranging between a minimum of £40 and a new top value of £60 according to the status of the race, out of which the second horse received £10 with £5 to the third. Starters were allowed free entry except for the winner and second, the usual entry fee of £1 or £2 (according to the value of the race) being applicable in the latter circumstance.

An intriguing press report of the second day's sport in 1901 reads,

"After taking the last flight of hurdles in the straight Shevian came a cropper and rolled right over on jockey W Oates. For a while the rider was rendered insensible but soon recovered consciousness and was carried back to the paddock on an improvised ambulance. Drs Johnson and Cappaidge found he had sustained concussion of the brain though not of a very serious nature and by the afternoon was practically himself."

One is bound to wonder as to what comprised "an improvised ambulance". I remember attending a point-to-point in the early 1950s which was held over a moorland course at Dunnabridge when an unconscious rider was transported by the use of a field gate as a stretcher, over the best part of a mile before reaching the nearest road.

The second day in 1903 was best remembered for the atrocious weather.

"A wretched storm burst over the course after the first race and the remainder of the meeting was as miserable as it is possible to contemplate. The rain powered down in torrents and before long comfort was out of the question. Not even the main grandstand provided any shelter and the course soon became deserted. The Somerset Steeplechase brought three runners and it proved a farce. The river was greatly swollen but horses and riders nevertheless ventured across it. Two of the three contestants came to grief, one of whom remounted twice to finish second. An objection was made to the winner for taking the jump in the home straight, but the stewards over-ruled the objection, taking into consideration that the other two horses both ran the wrong side of a flag."

Further noteworthy events are recorded in the Racing Calendar of 1910. In the Maiden Optional Selling Hurdle, first past the post Mr A M Crickett's

King Pepper was disqualified as he was on the forfeit list. In the following race Mr H Francis' Astrologer survived an objection from the third on the grounds that a contingency in the horse had not been registered, but the deposit money was returned. Leave to appeal was refused by the Acting Stewards, Sir Robert Harvey, Bt., Col. J A T Garratt, Mr L Densham and Mr W J Phillips. A dead heat occurred in the Somerset Steeplechase run over three miles, between Mr F J Farquharson's Escutcheon, ridden by his owner and Mr G Gully's Andora, ridden by Mr A Smith. The stakes of £40 to the winner and £15 to the second were divided. As far as I am able to ascertain dead heats at Totnes were a very rare occurrence notwithstanding the absence of the photo finish camera.

Yet another anomaly surfaced after the running of the fourth race. The Open Handicap Steeplechase over two miles. The Racing Calendar states,

"After the race for the Grand South Hams Steeplechase on the following (second) day, the Stewards, Col. J A T Garratt, Mr L Densham and Mr W J Phillips called upon the owner, Mr T Darke, the trainer, Mr E P Barthropp and jockey, J Woodman, for an explanation into the running of Conari in this race and not being satisfied with the same, reported the case to the Stewards of the National Hunt Committee, who accepted the explanations of owner, Mr T Darke and jockey Woodman, but were not satisfied with the explanation of Mr Barthropp and warned him off all courses where National Hunt Rules were in force. As it transpired that the horse had been entered by Mr Barthropp without registered authority from Mr Darke, the Stewards cautioned the latter to be more careful in the future."

Despite the incident-packed meeting of 1910, the previous year had also provided the management with problems, as the Somerset Steeplechase which required the river crossing, had to be confined to the Broadmarsh section of the track and with each circuit amounting to only six furlongs, the riders' mental calculations must have been fully stretched.

The 1911 meeting opened with two selling races. The first, a hurdle for horses which had not won a hurdle race, resulted in a walkover for the four year old Little Frankie owned by Mr G R Lawrence which was subsequently sold by auction for sixty-five guineas to Mr J A Clarke. The horse in its previous outing had finished as the runner up in another seller. The new connections obviously envisaged a quick return on their investment, for the animal turned out again on the second day in another selling hurdle, but despite starting favourite could finish no closer than in third place. The second seller on the card was a steeplechase which was won by Capt. C N Newton's Sexton in a three-horse contest. Sexton being a more valuable horse was bought in by his owner for ninety-one guineas. The horse had already scored at Devon & Exeter in his previous outing in a two horse non selling steeplechase. In fact the gelding had notched up six victories prior to his appearance at Totnes and to justify the owner's confidence in him Sexton finished first in his next four races. He faced the starter no less than twenty-seven times during the calendar year, winning eleven races, and towards the end of 1911 was also placed at Kempton Park and Gatwick Park before finishing first in the two mile Cleeve Selling 'Chase at Cheltenham. Here the subsequent bidding proved to be too hot for Capt. Newton and the horse was purchased by Mr G F Avila for 210 guineas, a goodly sum indeed for the winner of a selling race in those days, as all the owner received was £50, the advertised sale price, together of course with the prizemoney of £70. An interesting feature of this transaction was that Mr Avila was the owner of the second horse and as such, received half the surplus (over the selling price of £50) which amounted to a windfall of eighty guineas (see chapter including Rules and Regulations). There was, however, a sting in the tail for Mr Avila, owner of Henry II, as his horse was claimed by a Mr Pullen. This claim would have cost Mr Pullen £50 (the sale price) plus £70 being the value of the race, a total of £120. Yet another fascinating postscript to the Totnes race took place on October 12th at Monmouth races, a month later, when Capt. Newton's Sexton won the two mile selling steeplechase and was subsequently bought in by his owner. The Stewards observed that Capt. Newton had repeatedly interfered with a bidder, after the auctioneer had requested him to desist, and cautioned him as to his future behaviour. Noel Newton was the owner of a string of horses which on occasion he partnered himself with much success. He also acted as a Steward at Plymouth Races from time to time and appears a likely candidate for the 'poacher turned gamekeeper' nomination.

Only twenty-two runners faced the starter on the six race card on the first day of the 1912 fixture. The second day showed only a marginal improvement with twenty-six going to post.

The meeting was noteworthy for jockey W Rollason falling foul of the Stewards on both days with regard to his riding of Mr W Grieve's Hamilton which had finished third in a two mile hurdle race, beaten eight lengths by the winner on day one. The Stewards called Rollason before them together with the owner who was also the trainer, to explain his riding of Hamilton and, not being satisfied with his explanation, cautioned him as to his future riding. The next day, the horse, again partnered by Rollason, proceeded to win a similar race over the same distance, which obviously infuriated the Stewards as once again both men were called before them to explain the running of Hamilton compared to the previous day. Not being satisfied with the explanation they reported the matter to the Stewards of the National Hunt Committee. As a result of this referral, both men appeared before the Stewards of this Committee the following month to further explain the running of Hamilton when their explanations were accepted. They were either completely innocent of any wrong doing or had used the intervening month between referral and appearance, to get their stories in order.

In the years preceding the First World War owners had become less enthusiastic about running their horses at Totnes, with declining fields. The hazards on the course together with the river crossings were not so attractive as the value of their animals increased. In addition to the accidents which were the result of falls at the obstacles, horses were reported as having run into walls, disappeared into the river and having great difficulty negotiating the sharp right-hand bend after the winning post. Where once every steeplechase required a crossing of the Dart these were reduced to two on each day and in 1912 to just one. The last two such races resulted in a match and a walkover.

By today's standards, it is certain that Health and Safety officials would have had a field day at any racecourse of the era and there is also no doubt that the advent of plastic running rails and wings together with the abolition of concrete and stout wooden posts has been a major step forward in improving the safety of both horse and rider. In addition the present jockey's helmet with its safety straps ensure that it remains in place following a fall. The lightweight back and collar bone protector is another safety aid which was denied to jockeys of former times.

1878 racecard displaying 5 races

CHAPTER 5
RULES AND REGULATIONS

Each succeeding year brings changes or modifications to the Rules of Racing, yet many of the Regulations which were in force one hundred years ago have not changed dramatically and still provide the basis for those which are in place today. However, in the eighteenth and much of the nineteenth centuries there appear some which although 'of their time' would now be viewed as somewhat strange and impractical in today's world.

In 1848 a Committee Plate was advertised for a prize of ten sovereigns which comprised the running of heats on the flat, encompassing two circuits of the track and for which all entries were received on the day of the races. In addition, all ponies were to be entered on the course. An even earlier race programme was produced for the archives by Mr E Shinner of Stretchford Farm, Staverton, and is dated 1801. It is entitled "Totnes Annual Diversions" and lists the entries for three races together with the names and heights of the Ponies, Galloways and Hunters with the weights to be carried (except in the case of the Ponies, which may be assumed to be catchweights) Galloways were small stocky ponies between 13.0 hands and 15.0 hands, originally from Galloway in Scotland, hence their name, but generally applied to any animal that loosely fitted the description. Incidentally, members of the Shinner family are still in residence at Stretchford.

By 1873 the entry system had changed, with the announcement that all entries were to be made to the Clerk of the Course, at the Seymour Hotel before 8.30 p.m. on the day preceding the races. Five races were to be run each day, two over fences, one over banks, one hurdle race and one flat race on the first day and one over fences, two over banks, with one hurdle race and one flat race for the second day. An unusual Rule by today's standards stated that all handicaps were to be made by the Stewards, Clerk of the Course and Management Committee. I wonder how long and with what degree of agreement or perhaps acrimony that took to sort out? Further, that three horses must start for each race, except for hurdle races, for which there shall be four or the Public Money (presumably that contributed to the Race Fund by the Town) will not be given. This ruling was changed in later years. A rather drastic ground rule was in force that simply stated that "all dogs found on the course will be destroyed".

Regulations regarding admission charges included the pronouncement that all carriages remaining on the ground (overnight) were to pay on each day. Subscribers or non-subscribers of less than one guinea will be charged ten shillings and sixpence each. All prizes will be paid in specie and the tolls of the raceground will be let by auction at the Seymour Hotel (now divided into flats and apartments) the day prior to the first day's racing at 6.30 p.m. A personal favourite of all the ground rules listed is that, "Persons not riding in the colours entered will be fined ten shillings and sixpence and all riders must wear top boots and breeches".

Regulations as laid down a century ago by the National Hunt Committee with regard to the layout of the course required that there shall be in each mile at least one ditch six feet wide and two feet deep on the take off side of the fence, which ditch may be left open or guarded by a single rail, by a bank and rail, or by a bank only, not exceeding two feet in height and which fence must be at least four feet, six inches in height and if of dead brushwood or gorse, two feet in width. In all steeplechase courses there shall be, in the first two miles, at least twelve fences and in each succeeding mile at least six fences. A water jump of at least twelve feet wide and two feet deep, to be left open or guarded by a fence, not exceeding three feet in height. Not more than three feet of the minimum width of twelve feet of water can be allowed for shelving on the landing side.

In all hurdle races there shall not be less than six flights of hurdles in the first one and a half miles, with an additional flight for every quarter of a mile. The height of the hurdles should be not less than three feet, six inches from the bottom bar to the top bar. Devotees of present day National Hunt racing will recognise some familiar statistics in those measurements. The days of pony racing had now long gone as a Regulation categorically states that no Pony or Galloway race shall take place at any meeting held under these Rules.

I confess that I hold a fascination for the mechanics of the Selling Race, never more so when as a teenager I used to seek an advantageous position around the winner's enclosure immediately after the running of the race, so as to gain an uninterrupted view of the proceedings. In the era of Totnes Races the rules concerning selling races were different from those currently in force. The principal reason for change being that the modifications assisted in reducing the aggravation which frequently occurred between bidders and the owner and/or trainer of horses which although of moderate ability were not capable of being successful in any other grade of contest but nevertheless whose connections wished to retain ownership. In particular they did not react kindly to competition at the subsequent auction from the owner of the second horse, who in effect received a subsidy from the winner if his bid was successful. As may be imagined this state of affairs could and indeed did lead on occasion to bad blood and fisticuffs between the relevant parties. The modifications also permitted the winning owner to keep a portion of the surplus auction money above the entered sale price, which is now much fairer than of old. The rules for selling races relevant to the era read as follows:

"In all selling races the lowest selling price shall be no less than £50 (i.e. all that the owner received). In all selling races the winner shall be offered for sale by auction immediately after the race and the surplus, if any, over the entered selling price shall be divided equally between the owner of the second horse and the Race Fund. Any such sale by auction shall be subject to a right to bid for, or to buy in, such horse on behalf of the seller. All other horses starting may be claimed for the entered selling price, plus the value of the Stakes or Plate, by the owners of other horses running in the race or by their authorised agents. No person can claim more than one horse. In the case of a dead heat, the time for selling or claiming is postponed until the dead heat is run off or unless the owners agree to divide."

Many bargain buys have been made from the purchase of an animal from a seller whether through the auction or by way of a claim. Two post-war examples come to mind when Mr H R Morgan's Blow Horn which he had obtained from a selling 'chase, came good in the Welsh Grand National when prepared by Kingsbridge trainer, Mr Tommy Jarvis. Another acquisition in similar circumstances was Royal Sun, as the result of a seller at Buckfastleigh in 1949. Subsequently raced in local point-to-points and under National Hunt rules, the horse was the winner of twenty-three races. He was owned by Mr L Gerald Cottrell, who subsequently made a name for himself by training winning sprinters on the flat, only relinquishing his licence a few years ago. Probably the pinnacle of Royal Sun's achievements under National Hunt rules was the defeat of the well-known steeplechaser and Grand National contestant, Steel Lock (ridden by R Francis) in a three mile steeplechase at Buckfastleigh. During the current year in which I write (2009) a horse by the name of Mount Benger has scored six times, changing hands after his fourth victory in selling company with his final success for the year coming in a handicap 'chase at Cheltenham worth over £6,000 to the winner.

In 1904 one hundred and forty-nine jockeys held professional licences and sixty-five amateur riders including one who sported the eye-catching name of Chevalier de Kattendyke (I don't think that he ever appeared at Totnes). Professional licences cost £1 per year and these riders were allowed to compete in hunter steeplechases alongside their amateur cousins. Indeed most races under National Hunt Rules benefited from the talented amateur rider who held his own against professional rivals. The professionals earned a riding fee of ten guineas for winning a steeplechase or hurdle race of the advertised value of 100 sovereigns or upwards and to a losing jockey five guineas. In all other races (which applied to all of the West Country circuit at the time) the fees shall be five guineas and three guineas respectively. Jockeys could also claim travelling expenses plus £1 per day as livings costs. They were entitled to a riding allowance of 5lb. in weight if they had not won ten races. It was optional for a rider to weigh out or in, with his bridle and the Clerk of the Scales shall, if requested allow 1lb. for a curb or double bridle, but if a horse shall run in a hood, muzzle, martingale, breast plate or clothing, it must be put into the scale and included in a rider's weight. Whips, plates or anything worn on a horse's legs to be excepted.

As all well versed racegoers will know, the racehorse's official birthday is on 1st January no matter in what part of the year it is foaled. Every horse listed on the racecard or in the Racing Calendar that is over six years of age was described as 'aged', which without recourse to the General Stud Book it was not possible to identify a seven year old from a veteran of fifteen years or more. A century-old rule similar to one in force today is that no horse shall run under four years of age for a steeplechase, for a hurdle race until 1st September of the year in which he is three years old (slight variation here) nor for any race for which certificates from Masters of Hounds are required until 1st October of the year in which he is four years old. This latter condition ties in with the present situation regarding point-to-point racing. A regulation which is certainly not relative to present times, is one concerning a owner running two or more horses in the same race, who may declare to win with one of them, such declaration being made at scale. The rider of a horse, which an owner has not declared to win, must on no account stop such horse except in favour of the horse on whose behalf declaration to win has been made.

The rule concerning persons becoming involved with unlicensed racing remains today pretty much the same as it was then. Such meetings have throughout the centuries taken place on occasion. One of these occurred in 1912 at Bozomzeal and was known as Dittisham Races, run some half a dozen miles from Totnes. It comprised a six race card. The first of these was run over banks and a distance of two miles for which there were five entries with a silver cup to the winner, second receiving £3, third £2 and fourth £1. The second event was over the same course and confined to farmers over whose land the Britannia Beagles regularly hunt. There was an entry of eight. The third race was for ponies 13.0 hands high and under, limited to a six mile radius of the Royal Naval College, Dartmouth, over the same course. Prizes were a cup value three guineas to the winner, second 30 shillings, third 10 shillings fourth 5 shillings, only three entries. The fourth race was Open to all comers over an extended course of 2½ miles; prizes £4, £3 and £2 – four entries. In the fifth seven entries were to hand for prizes of a piece of plate value three guineas, £2, £1 and 10/-, this race being confined to followers of the Britannia Beagles over a distance of two miles. The final race was a flat race to be run in one field about 2½ miles which received six entries. The colours to be carried were listed in most cases with the occasional animal having 'For Sale' attached to its name. Unsurprisingly the names of the owners and officials are not familiar as being involved with the Totnes and Bridgetown Races. As a flavour we find listed Messrs J Trant, H Pearse, A H Pook, A Toms, S W Dusting, W Foale, W and T Ferris, C Foale, S V Moxon, J H H Owen, M M Hawke, F Waycott and the Misses Ivy and Vera Bond. Judges were G M Fleming, Esq. and H B Bartlett, Clerks of the

Course being A Toms, C Foale, W Edgeland and W Ferris. The Hon. Sec. was Mr J. Oldreive. From the race conditions it would seem that the Britannia Beagles and their supporters were major players in the organisation although no foot followers were catered for! The admission to the field was 6d with motors 2/6d, four-wheeled carriages 1/6d and two-wheeled 1 shilling, occupants at 6d each.

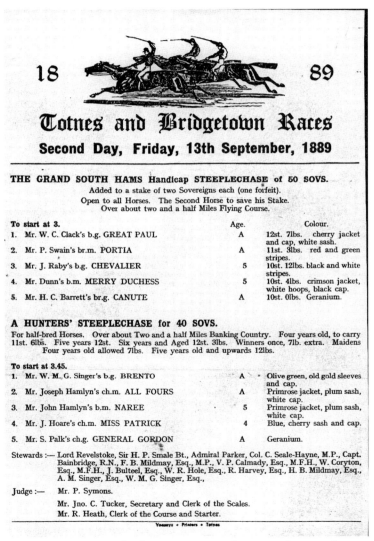

18 . 89

Totnes and Bridgetown Races

Second Day, Friday, 13th September, 1889

THE GRAND SOUTH HAMS Handicap STEEPLECHASE of 50 SOVS.

Added to a stake of two Sovereigns each (one forfeit).
Open to all Horses. The Second Horse to save his Stake.
Over about two and a half Miles Flying Course.

To start at 3.	Age.	Colour.
1. Mr. W. C. Clack's b.g. GREAT PAUL	A	12st. 7lbs. cherry jacket and cap, white sash.
2. Mr. P. Swain's br.m. PORTIA	A	11st. 3lbs. red and green stripes.
3. Mr. J. Raby's b.g. CHEVALIER	5	10st. 12lbs. black and white stripes.
4. Mr. Dunn's b.m. MERRY DUCHESS	5	10st. 4lbs. crimson jacket, white hoops, black cap.
5. Mr. H. C. Barrett's br.g. CANUTE	A	10st. 0lbs. Geranium.

A HUNTERS' STEEPLECHASE for 40 SOVS.

For half-bred Horses. Over about Two and a half Miles Banking Country. Four years old, to carry 11st. 6lbs. Five years 12st. Six years and Aged 12st. 3lbs. Winners once, 7lb. extra. Maidens Four years old allowed 7lbs. Five years old and upwards 12lbs.

To start at 3.45.		Colour.
1. Mr. W. M. G. Singer's b.g. BRENTO	A	Olive green, old gold sleeves and cap.
2. Mr. Joseph Hamlyn's ch.m. ALL FOURS	A	Primrose jacket, plum sash, white cap.
3. Mr. John Hamlyn's b.m. NAREE	5	Primrose jacket, plum sash, white cap.
4. Mr. J. Hoare's ch.m. MISS PATRICK	4	Blue, cherry sash and cap.
5. Mr. S. Palk's ch.g. GENERAL GORDON	A	Geranium.

Stewards :— Lord Revelstoke, Sir H. P. Smale Bt., Admiral Parker, Col. C. Seale-Hayne, M.P., Capt. Bainbridge, R.N., F. B. Mildmay, Esq., M.P., V. P. Calmady, Esq., M.F.H., W. Coryton, Esq., M.F.H., J. Bulteel, Esq., W. R. Hole, Esq., R. Harvey, Esq., H. B. Mildmay, Esq., A. M. Singer, Esq., W. M. G. Singer, Esq.,

Judge :— Mr. P. Symons.

Mr. Jno. C. Tucker, Secretary and Clerk of the Scales.

Mr. R. Heath, Clerk of the Course and Starter.

Vesseys • Printers • Totnes

Racecard 1889 – only the two principal races advertised

Jumping the water: spectators making use of the wall in the background
Photo courtesy of Totnes Image Bank & Rural Archive

In action, Cheviotdale (Mr A B Mildmay) - 1935, nearest camera

In the Paddock, Mr A B Mildmay aboard Cheviotdale - 1935

1938. The finish from the stands; Abbot's Glance (winner) followed home by The Ruff   Photo courtesy of Totnes Image Bank & Rural Archive

Sir Robert Harvey of Dundridge, Harberton, a Steward of the Races
Photo courtesy of Totnes Image Bank & Rural Archive

Mr H F Brunskill, M.F.H., (left) a Patron and Steward in conversation with Secretary Mr John Mason
Photo courtesy of Totnes Image Bank & Rural Archive

41

Above left, discussing the card. Amateur rider Mr G Bowden with Lady Normanton and Mrs G Archibald, 1938. Above right, Mr G Turner, a Steward and Mr A Hingston, Director.

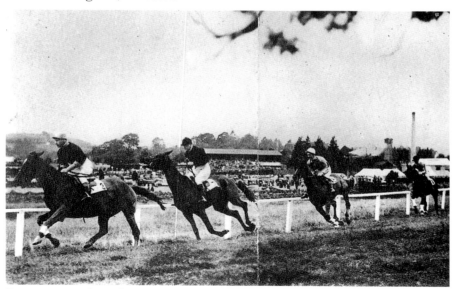

Runners rounding the turn into the back straight
Photo courtesy of Totnes Image Bank & Rural Archive

CHAPTER 6
PERSONAGES AND PERSONALITIES

Today, every racecourse has its appointed panel of Stewards which are often selected through a past association with an equestrian sport. Each recruit is then subject to an intensive training course with successful candidates being allocated to one or more racecourses. Annual seminars are held as 'refreshers' and for Stewards to be acquainted with changes or modifications to the regulations. During the times of Totnes and Bridgetown Races this was not so. Stewards were equipped with a book of rules and regulations and lacking modern day technology, the rest was based on common sense.

Totnes races throughout its history sported an impressive list of dignitaries who acted as Stewards, many of whose names were to be found in Debretts or 'Who's Who'. A high percentage were drawn from the hunting field, many of whom were at one time Masters of Hounds. The earliest reference discovered lists Mr J B Y Buller as the sole Steward in 1848. Two years later he had been replaced by Mr W B Fortescue and in 1851 it was Mr Henry Carew. Lord Seymour also took his turn and frequently donated the sum of fifty pounds to a Plate which was the principal race for the day. Mr C B Baldwin, described as 'a fine old sportsman' also gave fifty pounds to a race on the second day of the meeting, on which he was a Steward. The main event on each day was for a purse, the gift of some local gentleman, usually a Steward of the meeting. In 1856 two names appeared. In addition to Mr Fortescue we find Mr E Scobell. The 1873 racecard contains the names of Rt. Hon. Lord Churston, and Mr J Carpenter-Garnier, M.P. It is more than likely that J B Y Buller (1848) and Lord Churston are one and the same gentleman as Yarde Buller was the family name. Five Stewards were appointed in 1885: Earl Poulett, Earl Buchan, Lord Cardross, Admiral the Honourable Sir H Keppel and Major Trist. Racecards of 1888 and 1889 display a greatly enlarged panel. The first year names six stewards: Count de Morel, Col. C Seale-Hayne, M.P., F B Mildmay, M.P., W R Hole, Esq., A M Singer, Esq. and W M G Singer, Esq. and the following year the original six were joined by Lord Revelstoke, Sir H P Seale, Bt., Admiral G Parker, Capt. J H Bainbridge, R.N., A.D.C. (who later became a Rear Admiral), W. Coryton, M.F.H., V. P. Calmady, M.F.H., J. Bulteel, Esq., R Harvey, Esq. (later to become Sir Robert Harvey) and H B Mildmay, Esq. The Racing Calendar shows that just three would have been selected to adjudicate at any enquiry.

From the above panel Col. C Seale-Hayne was a Member of Parliament and his name has been perpetuated up to the present time by his donation of property on the outskirts of Newton Abbot to be used for educational purposes in relation to agriculture and is known as Seale-Hayne College. Many students have obtained graduation status at the College which has recently closed with much controversy. Lord Revelstoke was a member of the well-known Baring family who were bankers. Mr V P Calmady was the Master of the Tetcott Foxhounds and others who were or became Masters of Foxhounds were Admiral George Parker of Delamore, Ivybridge (Dartmoor Foxhounds), his son-in-law Mr William Coryton who held two Masterships, firstly the East Cornwall Foxhounds followed by the Dartmoor. He was known affectionately as "the Squire". Mr Henry B Mildmay and his son, Mr Francis B Mildmay, the latter being the Member of Parliament for Totnes, resided at Flete and the family were to play such important roles in horseracing in future years. Mr John Bulteel of Pamflete was the son of Mr John Crocker Bulteel, another Master of the Dartmoor Hunt, and the head of another dynasty that was to leave an indelible mark in racing circles. John Bulteel was the father of both John George and Walter Bulteel who we shall encounter in due course.

Mr A M Singer and Mr W M G Singer were members of the illustrious American family of sewing machine fame. Both were well known racehorse owners and great supporters of Totnes Races and its neighbouring tracks. Indeed their horses represented them throughout the country although having little luck with their runners in the Grand National. Mr Washington Singer's racing colours were olive green, with gold sleeves and cap. Although he did not register any successes in the major races under National Hunt Rules, he gained a notable win on the flat, when his colt, Challacombe, won the 1905 St. Leger, the horse named after the Dartmoor hamlet which is situated near Grimspound. Following his death in 1934 his wife's colours of myrtle green with white striped sleeves and white cap continued to appear on racecourses up to and including the 1950s when I recall a horse in her ownership finishing second in a hurdle race at Newton Abbot. Mr Singer was at one time a pupil at Totnes Grammar School and a major benefactor of Totnes Races with presentations of both trophies and prize money. He lived at Streatfield, Paignton,and became a Master of the South Devon Hunt. His family were responsible for the building of several fine houses in the area, especially Oldway Mansion at Paignton. He also purchased the Leigham estate at Ilsington to add to his impressive portfolio.

Mr Robert Harvey was succeeded by his son, Sir Samuel Harvey of Dundridge, Harberton, some two miles from the town. The Duke of Somerset, a member of the Seymour family with estates in and around Totnes, Major O H Green who was Master of the Dartmoor Otterhounds and Mr Harold St. Maur were soon to join the panel. Mr St. Maur was a Master of the South Devon Hunt and held a commission with the 14th Hussars which he resigned in order to return to the locality to live at Stover and administer his estates also to enjoy his sporting interests. All three of these gentlemen were to be appointed as Stewards approaching the end of the nineteenth century replacing some of the older generation as they approached retirement. Col. J A G Garratt, Master of the East Devon was also the founder of the hunt in 1890 and he was soon followed by Mr J G Bulteel, son of Mr John Bulteel. Known as George Bulteel he was to cut a mighty figure in horse racing circles. Mr Hubert F Brunskill was yet another well known Master of Foxhounds. His initial venture into a Mastership was with the South Pool Harriers whilst residing at Buckland Tout Saints before transferring to take control of the Exmoor Foxhounds. From there he reverted to more familiar surroundings by his appointment as Master of the South Devon Foxhounds. In later years he moved to Glazebrook, near South Brent. Mr Leigh Densham was another local recruit, being a long time Master of the Dart Vale Harriers in whose hunting country the racecourse lies.

In the years leading up to the Second World War, and the demise of Totnes races, Major F H B Passy of Blatchford, Cornwood, appeared on the panel and was a well known member of the Dartmoor Hunt. The names of many of these Stewards were also to be seen listed at neighbouring courses such as Buckfastleigh, Newton Abbot, Torquay, South Brent and Plymouth. I have left until last, mention of the Steward who lived within a stone's throw of the course itself. A long time servant to the races was Mr Walter J Phillips, whose residence, The Mount, is situated within a mile of the race course and he would have been ideally placed to be called upon to carry out an early morning inspection! Mr Phillips was at the time Master of the Dart Vale Harriers.

Before the advent of the railway in 1847 nearly all the horses which competed at Totnes were locally owned and trained, transportation being the key factor. Farmers kept the odd thoroughbred, chiefly for hunting purposes, before graduating to the local point-to-point. These types of races were fewer and further between than at the time of writing. In the 1920s only eleven were included in the calendar for the Devon and Cornwall area. These were the East Cornwall, North Cornwall, Dartmoor, East Devon, Dulverton, Haldon Harriers, Lamerton, 'Mr Spooners' Harriers, Silverton, Tetcott, South Tetcott and Tiverton as opposed to the twenty-nine meetings of the current year. The more adventurous owner would then be tempted to try his luck at the professional game (owners were chiefly of the male sex) if they believed that they owned an animal with some ability. There were others who were either gentlemen of means or 'well to do' tradesmen who were extremely supportive of the Devonshire circuit with their charges.

Three from the latter category were members of the Hamlyn family from Buckfastleigh. Their residence and training establishment was at Fullaford House where at times ten or a dozen horses were housed. Their influence was to be seen on the local courses throughout the final decade of the nineteenth century and the early years of the twentieth. John Hamlyn, together with his sons John and Joseph, were the directors of Hamlyn Brothers who were woollen manufacturers and tanners. The woollen business was established at

Buckfastleigh with the tanneries together with a woollen trade at Horrabridge and Liskeard. John Hamlyn died in 1899 at the early age of forty-nine years. The family were devotees of field sports, racing, hunting and shooting and were benefactors of several sporting clubs. Their list of horses included Haste, Eclipse, Sainfoin, Caprice, Student, Lord Tennyson, Miss Ivy, Vanity, Reprieve, Decadence, Hurry II, Bogus, St. Selskar, Discord, Port Erin, Homestead and Precital, all of whom carried their silks between 1897 and 1903, several being multiple winners. Their familiar colours of primrose jacket with plum sleeves and a white cap were as prominent on the South West circuit as those of Alfred Renfree in the 1950s and 1960s.

Among the smaller training enterprises was Richard Ferris from Capton, Dittisham. There were two persons of that name who were father and son. Ferris Jnr. was a member of the Royal College of Veterinary Surgeons and officiated in that capacity at Buckfastleigh Races where at one time he was also the starter. His father kept a hunting and racing stable. He was a well known follower of hounds and continued to be seen aboard his thoroughbreds at the age of eighty-eight years. Two of his racehorses were appropriately named Capton Rose and South Devon whilst others in his ownership were Ceres and Commander. Another well known performer that was locally owned was Mr E B Oldrieve's Ruby's Darling. The mare was to be seen with great regularity on the South Western circuit, nearly always giving a good account of herself. Mr John H Glover farmed at Ivybridge and his representatives on the racecourse in the early part of the twentieth century were Golden Sunshine, Blink Bonny, Despatch, Young Tom, Kilbride and Texas. All three of these stables, Messrs Ferris, Oldrieve and Glover, produced the occasional winner.

Charles Gregor was a professional trainer and jockey as well as owning a few horses. He was based at the Manor House (now Church House), South Brent. Like the Hamlyn stable at Buckfastleigh, being situated on the edge of Dartmoor, both outfits made use of the moor on which they established their gallops. The area used by Charlie Gregor was for many years after his demise still known as "Gregor's Gallops". His stable was 'very small beer' compared to that of the Hamlyns, but nevertheless in 1909 his horse, Masy won a steeplechase on each day of the two-day Totnes meeting although not partnered by himself but by Walter Bulteel. It is possible that he had retired from race riding at that stage to concentrate on his training. Much support for Totnes Races came from local owners and the following names of Messrs Michelmore, Pethick, Pearse, Sandover, Smerdon, Hoare, Holman, Partridge and Hawker are still to be found in the County.

There is no doubt that the most well known and influential owner of the decade was George Bulteel. His support of his local tracks with numerous horses was legendary at the time and his runners were well supported in the ring for good reason as they were frequently to be seen in the winner's enclosure. The two-day fixture in 1901 was a typical example of what transpired. A newspaper at the time reported that, "There was a fair duel in the Totnes Hurdle Race between Mr Agar's Little Cicestrian and Mr J G Bulteel's Snarley Yow but the latter, a decided favourite, always had something in hand and came away strongly in the home straight. Mr Bulteel secured a double victory by carrying off the second event on the card, the Bridgetown Steeplechase with Euphresia who was the easiest of winners. What should have been the race of the day the Dart Vale Steeplechase, for which the biggest stake was offered, resolved itself into a match between Mr J G Bulteel's North Sea and Mr J Blake's Boa, only these two completing out of eight entries starting. It was certainly a rare match and produced the best finish of the day. Boa on whom the odds were laid passed the Judge's box a neck ahead but was disqualified for going the wrong course by taking the water jump in the second round, although leave was given to appeal."

The second day's review included the following newspaper quotation, "Mr J G Bulteel secured his third win of the meeting by carrying off the first event on the card with Tennebrosa although only after the favourite had had a desperate tussle with Mr Parker's Lady Sophie." This was a selling hurdle with the winner who was only a four year old being bought in for 155 guineas, a fair sum in those days. Connections must have realised the potential of their winner as the gelding proceeded to gain two further successes in non-sellers in his next two outings at Plymouth and Hawthorn Hill. The greatest triumph for George Bulteel came to fruition many miles away from Totnes, as the owner of the great steeplechaser, Manifesto, whose exploits at Aintree in the Grand National were unsurpassed until Red Rum appeared on the scene, some seventy-five years later. I make no apology for listing a brief synopsis of his achievements.

The horse was bred by Mr H M Dyas and it was in his ownership that he made his first attempt at the National at the age of seven, finishing in fourth place in 1895. The next year he fell at the first fence in a field of twenty-eight in the race won by The Soarer ridden by Mr David Campbell. In 1897 Manifesto came into his own when, ridden by T Kavanagh, he secured victory by 20 lengths. The horse was unable to revisit Aintree the following year as he escaped from his box, jumped a five-bar gate and rapped his fetlock so badly that he was unable to run for several months. It was at this stage that Mr George Bulteel appeared on the scene. He had heard a rumour that Mr Dyas was prepared to sell his horse and as Mr Bulteel was seeking a live candidate for the big race, the deal was done with Manifesto returning to Aintree in 1899. This time the horse was burdened with top weight of 12st. 7lb., 18lb., more than he carried to victory two years previously, and was ridden by George Williamson. Taking up the running three fences from home he won by an easy five lengths, giving the second horse 25lb. The next year in finishing third, he probably put up his best ever performance and the best to have been seen in the history of the race. Carrying the crushing burden of 12st. 13lb. he was beaten four lengths and a neck by Ambush II and Barsac, giving 24lb. to the winner and 37lb. to the second.

Manifesto did not take part in the Grand National of 1901 and did not race at all that season but returned in 1902 when fourteen years of age carrying 12st. 8lb. once again being placed third behind Shannon Lass and Matthew to whom he was conceding 35lb. and 38lb. respectively, the distances being three lengths and the same. In the Grand Sefton (at Aintree) he carried 12st. 12lb. finishing second to Kirkland who was receiving 35lb. At fifteen years of age the handicapper relented somewhat dropping his weight to a mere 12st. 3lb. in 1903. Once again the gallant old horse finished third to Drumcree. George Bulteel also ran another horse, Deershayes, who fell. At sixteen years of age Manifesto returned for the National of 1904 carrying what was for him the feather weight of 12st. 1lb. and finished eighth. This was to be his swansong in the Grand National but he did return to Aintree the following November to run and complete the course once again, in the Valentine Steeplechase. After eight appearances in the big race his retirement had been well earned. Manifesto earned a prize of £1,975 when winning his first National and the same sum for his second triumph.

The Grand National was the premier steeplechase in the country and was more highly rated than the Cheltenham Gold Cup as we are able to appreciate from the following comparisons of prizemoney. The Gold Cup was not competed for until 1924 although I have discovered that a Gold Cup race of sorts was run over a hundred years previously: 1924 Gold Cup – value to winner £685, Grand National - £8,240; 1936 Gold Cup - £670, Grand National - £7,095; 1950 Gold Cup - £2,936-10-0, Grand National - £9,314; and in 1956 Gold Cup - £3,750-5-0, Grand National £8,695, which illustrates that the Cheltenham race was very much the poor relation.

A visitor to Totnes in the years preceding the First World War was Mr Oswald Mosley who became the leader of the British Union of Fascists, commonly known as the Blackshirts at the time of World War Two. He scored a double with his horses Tavora and Duplicate but as those with long memories or have recourse to the history books will know he was later to become much reviled as were his followers.

Mr Walter Bulteel, the brother of George, was a distinguished amateur rider as well as an owner. Amateur riders were abundant right from the early days of racing at Totnes. They showed a high degree of skill and competence and were rightly in demand by owners and trainers eager to secure their services. The more popular soon lost any claim to a weight allowance which had been due to them from the outset. A trio of horses, in his ownership were Gussy, Blagent and Cheshire. He partnered his first winner at Torquay races in 1896 and was soon to gain a reputation of some stature. After the turn of the century he joined the professional yard of Arthur Yates and rode eighty-six winners in the two years 1905 and 1906, which included the remarkable feat of riding in eleven of the twelve races at the Torquay Easter meeting of 1905, winning nine races and dead-heating for second place in another. He rode Baron de Forest's Lord Rivers in the 1909 Grand National, finishing fourteenth, and in the next year, Wickham, who failed to complete. He had previously finished eighth on Drumcree in 1906.

It should be noted that the Grand National fences of the time and for over the first half of the twentieth century bear only a passing resemblance to those in current use. The original jumps were upright and forbidding with deeper drops and were of a far more challenging nature to man and beast. Another well-known amateur of the day was Mr H W (Jack) Tyrwhitt-Drake. He was a frequent visitor to the West Country and crowned the 1911 season by becoming the Champion Amateur rider with fifty winners.

Steeplechasing has and always will be a hazardous occupation for a jockey,many having lost their lives as the result of falls on the racecourse. In my lifetime I have seen the demise of such well respected professionals as Fred O'Connor, Ivor Beckinsale, Mick Pumfrey and Douglas Barratt, plus Mr Alan Moule and Mr John Thorne. Two further amateur riders of the time met the same fate. Mr Herbert S Sidney died following a fall at Dunstall Park on Boxing Day 1902 aged thirty-one years through being struck by a following horse. His obituary stated that,

"Mr Sidney's untimely end will be regretted nowhere more than in the West of England, where he was known to a very large circle of sportsmen. For many seasons he has been a prominent figure at Plymouth, Totnes, Torquay, Newton Abbot and other Devon racecourses and was popular both as an owner and rider. He was a skilful steeplechase and hurdle rider and always got the utmost out of his mount. In 1900 he tied with Mr A W Wood with forty-nine winners as the leading amateur and was the outright winner the following year with fifty-one victories from one hundred and forty-nine rides."

An interesting comment was made by an eye witness to the accident who volunteered his opinion 'that jockeys ride too far forward when taking jumps. If the deceased had ridden with a straight back, the pecking of the horse would have landed him just above his seat instead of throwing him off'. I wonder what the witness would have thought of present day riding styles?

The second fatality occurred on the third day of the 1869 Totnes fixture, the victim being Mr George Barrett. It was reported that he was fatally injured as the result of a fall from Mr Coles' Gamecock after crossing the river and died at 5.a.m. the next morning. The Barrett family were located at Puddiford, near Totnes, and George was one of four brothers, Alfred, Thomas and Charles being siblings. Their father was described as a colt breaker so it was not unreasonable to assume that the sons were excellent riders.

From the professional ranks of jockeys recurring names were the brothers T and J Heath, Jack Woodman, E (Ned) Southwood and R (Bobby) Gordon. Bobby Gordon was a great favourite with the local racegoers and for good reason. On the second day of the 1910 meeting he rode a hat-trick of winners on the course and in the same year won nine of the twelve races at the two-day Easter event at Torquay also finishing second and third plus a fall in the remaining three: truly a remarkable record.

Probably not much notice was taken when a certain Ernest Piggott rode the winner of the Dart Vale Open Handicap Steeplechase in 1902 for Mr George Bulteel, on Greybridge, but Ernie Piggott was to strike up a good relationship with the Bulteel runners and was associated with his hat trick of winners Tenebrosa, Snarley Yow and Euphrasia. Piggott was to become a three times Champion Jockey and rode over five hundred winners. No one could have guessed what fate had in store for the future generations of this family, for his two sons, Victor and Keith and for his grandson, Lester. Ernie Piggott went on to win two Grand Nationals on Jerry M and Poethlyn.

Another family to wield great influence at the turn of the century were the Anthony siblings. Three jockey brothers all commenced their race riding careers as amateur riders before turning professional. Jack, Ivor and Owen were part of a family of seven brothers and six sisters. A younger brother, Gwynne, was to become the fourth member to try his hand as a rider but never achieved the same distinction as his more illustrious brothers. Ivor Anthony rode a double at Totnes in 1907 aboard Mr J T Longworth's Greenfinch in the Somerset Steeplechase and Mr G. Pennar's Apex in the Dart Vale Handicap 'Chase. A press report stated, "Ivor Anthony, the rider of Greenfinch, appeared to be the only one to be thoroughly conversant with the course and taking the right route won with something to spare".

In 1912 riding Mr D. Harrison's Fleacatcher he secured the two mile Handicap Steeplechase on successive days. Although not considered at the time to be the equal of his younger brother, Jack, Ivor was to finish third in the Grand National of three occasions: 1912, 1917 and 1918. He was subsequently to make his mark as a trainer, saddling Kellsboro Jack to win the 1933 Grand National and repeating the feat with Royal Mail in 1937. He was also the trainer of Morse Code which took the 1938 Cheltenham Gold Cup at the expense of Golden Miller, thus ending the great horse's sequence of five successive victories and being the only horse to beat "The Miller" at Cheltenham. Ivor Anthony completed a Gold Cup double with Poet Prince in 1941.

Jack Anthony was to win the Grand National as an amateur rider on three different horses: Glenside (1911), Ally Sloper (1915) and Troytown (1920). As a professional he finished second in 1925 and again in 1926 and third in 1927. As a trainer he was responsible for Easter Hero's victory in the Cheltenham Gold Cup of 1930.

Owen Anthony, the third brother to ride at Totnes, like Ivor was not able to scale the heights of Jack but nevertheless was placed second on Irish Mail in the National of 1913. He too made his mark as a trainer, succeeding Basil Briscoe as the handler of Golden Miller in 1936 when the horse collected his fifth Gold Cup, previously having trained Music Hall to succeed in the 1922 Grand National.

Mr Aubrey Hastings was yet another talented amateur to visit Broadmarsh in 1905 enjoying considerable riding honours. On the first day he rode a treble on Little Tom, Chaplin and The Chief. Little Tom and The Chief were pulled out again on the second day, both obliging for their connections and providing a five timer for Mr Hastings. The next year, 1906, saw Aubrey Hastings steer Ascetic's Silver to victory in the Grand National. Like many fine horsemen it was no surprise when he took out a trainer's licence which he used to good effect by turning out Ally Sloper, nine years after his riding achievement to add his name to the few who have both ridden and trained the winner of the National. The Hon. Aubrey Hastings, to accredit him with his full title, trained a large string of horses at Wroughton in Wiltshire and his winner was partnered by Mr Jack Anthony. Another patron of the Hastings yard was Prince Franz Hatzfeldt, an international sportsman, whose all yellow colours were carried to victory on several occasions at Totnes. It was fitting that upon the sudden death of Mr Hastings in 1929 the training establishment was taken over by Ivor Anthony. His future exploits with Brown Jack both over hurdles and on the flat became legendary. He was an amazing horse for any new trainer to inherit.

One professional jockey who will undoubtedly have remembered visiting Totnes races was W Daniels. His mount, Santella, was a runner in the Totnes Flying Steeplechase and lying in second place when stumbling in the river on the run home the pair were swept downstream. In addition to receiving a good ducking Daniels collected a cut to his head. No permanent or lasting damage can have been done because fourteen years later (1887) he won the Grand National aboard Gamecock. At a later fixture a well-known gentleman rider was to have been seen wading around in the river, looking like a drowned rat seeking his whip and pitifully exclaiming, "I came here to ride not to swim!" Another jockey who had accepted an engagement to ride at Totnes thought better of it when he learned that it involved two crossings of the river.

The most familiar name to be found on Totnes racecards of the nineteenth century and early twentieth was Heath. Richard Heath was appointed as Clerk of the Course in 1870, succeeding his father who had held the position for the previous twenty-one years. He in turn followed his father as Clerk, who had held that office for many years. (I have not been able to trace an initial date for this appointment.) Dick Heath was listed as the third generation of his family to take charge of the preparation and presentation of the racecourse. He was to remain in office for the next forty years. One report from the time suggests that Dick Heath was in fact the fourth generation of his family to have occupied the role and that his great grandfather was in situ from the start with the Heath name being associated with Totnes Races for over one hundred years. Dick also acted as the starter at Plymouth Races. He kept in his possession a letter received by him in 1905 from Lord Churston which read, "Please accept the enclosed as a memento of old times. I send it to you as I know what a keen interest your family have taken from time immemorial, in our little meeting, which my old friend, Heath (Richard's father) of the Seven Stars, used to describe as the 'Derby of the West'. His Lordship's enclosure, neatly mounted on card, was an advertisement which appeared in an Exeter paper on August 27th 1836, giving details of the Totnes and Bridgetown Races due three days later.

In 1902 it became necessary for Clerks of the Course, Judges, Starters and Handicappers to become licensed. Dick Heath was the first in Devon to be granted a Clerk's permit. In an interview with a local journalist he recollected receiving a letter from a gentleman in London, requesting information about a silver cup which was in his possession dated 1775. Unfortunately the Heath records did not extend as far as that date but he recalled that in 1834 "old John Horsley of Plymouth" won a gold cup at Totnes on a horse called The Tory. He spoke of the days before the introduction of racecards when there were 'penny lists'. These were printed plainly on slips of paper and distributed for a penny each. A list dated 31st August 1847 showed only three entry races and an odd one – a purse of three sovereigns for hacks. The next year in August 1848 Mr Derry's chestnut mare, My Mary, ran in the race for the prize of fifty sovereigns but was beaten by a bay gelding known as The Baronet. The Derry colours were amber jacket with a black cap.

By 1909 the Race Committee felt that some recognition of Dick Heath's services should be made. At the time he was the oldest Clerk of the Course in England. It was decided that a testimonial should be presented and a subscription list, limited to a maximum donation of one guinea, be opened with contributions to be collected by the Secretary, Mr A Hingston. Promises received were from the Duke of Somerset, Sir Robert Harvey, Mr F B Mildmay M.P., Mr Alfred Michelmore, Mr W J Phillips, Mr Charles Swears, Mr George Mitchell, Mr William Coryton, M.F.H., Mr G Sanders Davies, Mr Oxley Durant Parker, Mr Walter Cooper, Mr Standish Jackson, Mr Walter Roberts, Mr Elias Bishop; from Mr R F Marshall the sum of fifteen shillings, Capt. Adams (ten shillings and sixpence), The Mayor of Totnes (ten shillings), Mr T H Edmonds (ten shillings) and Mr H F Prince (ten shillings). The local press records that at the subsequent presentation, "a handsome purse of forty sovereigns was accepted with gratitude by Dick Heath who still lives in the quaint, homely and remarkably comfortable cottage in which both he and his father were born, in Fore Street."

Dick Heath was to remain as Clerk a further three years and was to literally die in harness at the age of sixty-eight. His obituary stated that he was normally a man of strong physique but that his constitution had been broken down in recent years by an insidious internal cancer. The month before his demise he had still been able to carry out his duties as Clerk of the Course at the Races, completing forty-three years of service. In addition to being the Starter at Plymouth Races, having attended that meeting for over fifty years, he had acted as Clerk of the Course or Starter at Torquay, Buckfastleigh and South Brent. He was a good horseman and rode at Totnes Races as far back as 1862, also in his youth at Torquay and Newton Abbot. He had many a fall over banks but escaped without broken bones. With the reputation of being an excellent raconteur and having a vivid memory of past events, he possessed an excellent collection of old race programmes, cards and lists. He had few outside interests but did serve two terms on the Town Council. He left a widow, a son and a daughter who was married to Mr R Parker, son of the then well-known owner of racehorses.

Mr Carew's Miss Oxnard leading Baffity (winner) in Somerset Handicap Steeplechase, circa 1902

CHAPTER 7
THE COMMITTEE TO 1914

Before the foundation of the Company, racing at Totnes was run by a Committee of prominent local men. I am unable to discover any records of Committee meetings prior to 1860, except for the occasional early references which I have included in previous chapters.

The 1860 Committee was comprised of the following members: Messrs Thomas Michelmore, Jeffrey Michelmore, Charles J Michelmore, John Heath, G H Cole, J Bowden Jnr., J Fogwill, William Willis (Surveyor), Samuel Heath (Clerk of the Course) and George Mitchell Snr. (Secretary). During the next twenty years other names to appear were Messrs James Pock, Thomas Holman, George Huxham, James Gill, William Gillard, William Hannaford, John Reddle, R Bourne, L Harris, T C Kellock, T E Owen, John Hamlyn, Samuel Cuming, Herman Taylor, John Blackaller and John Maye, the latter departing after just one year's service.

In the same year a dispute arose between the Committee and a Mr Willcocks, the purchaser of the race tolls, in that he was alleged to have breached the terms and conditions by not having erected a 'good and sufficient stand' before 1st September as specified. The Committee as a consequence decided to take the course into their own hands and collect the tolls themselves, Mr Willcocks forfeiting his payment. However, it was resolved that provided Mr Willcocks pay the money expended by the Committee in the erection of the stand, "so rendered necessary by his neglect", the income from the stand and the tolls would be handed over to him for his benefit. This did not satisfy Mr Willcocks who issued a writ which was contested by the Committee, with the result that the action would be tried at the forthcoming assizes. No result was recorded, only the settlement of the solicitor's account!

A different problem arose two years later with regard to the running of the Totnes Steeplechase. The winner 'Aunt Sally' was deemed to have passed on the wrong side of the winning post whilst the second home, 'Little Dan', was not qualified having already won a race to the value of £20 but that 'Pugelist' placed third, was properly qualified and entitled to the stakes. 'Aunt Sally' had also won the Grand South Hams Steeplechase and was fully entitled to that prize.

1863 saw the main grandstand built on the 'streats' with the second stand having sufficient space under and behind for weighing and that the weighing house measure 13ft. by 12ft. with a separate room for jockeys to dress, to be 10ft. square, somewhat cramped by today's standards.

Mr Evans, a shopkeeper in Totnes, sought permission to have Mr Dent's piece of plate placed in his window for exhibition purposes but this was rejected and that it should remain in the possession of the Secretary until the two race days when it would be on display at the grandstand. The Surveyor was instructed to level that part of the course that runs from the entrance to the Marsh to the finishing straight as he deemed necessary.

Diplomacy was much in evidence in 1865, when the Mayor of Totnes, Mr J F F Phillips, was invited to be a Steward whilst in the same year a letter was received from Messrs Broom and Mortimer stating that they would not permit the Marsh occupied by them to be used in any way for racing in consequence of Mr Robert Harris objecting to their names being retained on the list of voters for the Borough of Totnes. Presumably an amicable solution was found as racing went ahead.

Because of the huge increase in railway traffic – the *Totnes Times* reported that there were six or seven monster excursion trains during the day, all heavily freighted – the Committee petitioned the Great Western and South Western Rail Company to carry horses at a reduced rate as some owners were prevented from using this means of transport because of the cost. It would seem that the plea fell upon deaf ears as the request was not granted.

The Committee who arranged the erection and dismantling of the two temporary grandstands were also responsible for the annual letting of the tolls, Mr J Richardson being a regular purchaser. Each year a sub-committee was formed to act as handicappers to assess the weights to be carried by each entry in such races. A Town or Military Band was engaged to provide the music during the afternoon, which was often preceded by marching through the town before making their way to the bandstand which had been constructed on the course. However in 1876 heavy rain saw the cancellation of the morning parade.

The previous year twenty policemen had been employed to maintain law and order and four years later the number had increased to thirty-six. Their presence would appear to have been effective as three men, John Binmore, George Farley and John Ward, appeared before the Magistrates charged with assaulting P.C. Butt on the racecourse. The Constable had found a four year old child in a dangerous position in one of the booths, as a group of men and women were drunk and swaying over the child. In trying to extract the youngster, the policeman was set upon and 'ruffled'. The accused were fined ten shillings each. In 1877 John Jones was sentenced to six months hard labour for the theft of a purse containing twenty-three pounds. He had to face the charge without a defence as no solicitor in Totnes would handle his case. A few years later the press reported that the light-fingered gentry plied their craft with some success, several people being relieved of their purses and other possessions. Among these was Mr Jackman of Plymouth, who whilst in the grandstand was robbed of his purse containing several pounds and Mr Langworthy of Plymouth who lost a gold chain and spade guinea to which was attached a silver watch.

In 1877 William Kinder received one month's imprisonment for gambling on the course with small painted dice and Charles Stephens was sentenced to six weeks hard labour for gambling with a roulette wheel which he was able to stop as he chose.

There were many attractions which appeared on Broadmarsh. In 1875 they included a small menagerie, Lawrence's Models (whatever they may have been), the American Giant Horses, Dwarves, Lismore's Shooting Gallery, Boxing booths, Day's Cosmoramic Exhibition, Waller's Star Ghost Illusions, Miss Wallace the heaviest woman ever exhibited (no weight given) but Master Smith did weigh in at thirty-five stones.

In 1877 consideration was given to the erection of a bridge across Hempston Lake. At a subsequent meeting of the Committee it was agreed to accept the tender of Mr J Elliott to carry out the work for the sum of £6. Mr W J Tanner was requested to take money at the Paddock and Mr J Heath was paid £5 in compensation for damage done to Heart's Field by people passing to and from the Penny Bridge, this being the means by which anyone approaching the course from the railway would gain admittance. Needless to say, in due course, the Penny Bridge would become the victim of inflation. Since 1869 the race meeting had been a two-day fixture instead of the usual three.

A Deputy Secretary was appointed in 1879 in the person of Mr John C Tucker. He succeeded Mr Edwin Heath in the position, Heath also being the Clerk of the Scales. 1882 brought several changes to the Committee: Mr John Tucker was appointed as Secretary, Mr Robert Bourne resigned and Mr Sidney Paige Adams who had only been a member for a short time tendered his resignation upon leaving Totnes. New recruits were Mr Augustus Hingston, Mr Thomas Maye, Mr W H Punchard, Dr Raby, Mr George Mitchell Jr., and Mr R Nicholls, with Mr W F Tollitt as Surveyor to the Committee. Meetings were held at one of three venues: the Seymour Hotel, the Seven Stars and occasionally at Gate House.

By 1880 prices had started to increase. The cost of erecting the bridge across Hempston Lake together with the Paddock amounted to £19. Tolls which had previously been let by tender were now being sold by auction. Amounts realised in 1877 totalling £257 had risen to £380 just three years later. It was decided to increase the cost of admission to the grandstands by sixpence, with the main stand now priced at four shillings per person and the second stand, half-a-crown. It was also resolved that no saddle horses be allowed on the ground except those used by the Committee and officials.

It was agreed that the grandstand be carpeted and that estimates should be obtained for taking water from the water jump to Hempston lake by shute; also that the Clerk of the Course be granted permission to employ a man to assist in the 'weighing house' on race days. The Committee received an objection to the three runners in the Hunter Steeplechase of 1881 which they referred to the Stewards of the National Hunt Committee. They adjudicated that the race be declared void. The deposit paid by the objector Capt. Otway was returned, also the entry fees. Permission was sought on a yearly basis, from the Great Western Railway, for the public to cross the tramway. Likewise Buckfastleigh Railways were similarly approached for permission to use a piece of land adjoining the tramway for the purpose of erecting the grandstand. Other permissions were required from owners/tenants of land on the Bourton side of the river.

It would seem that Mr Sidney Paige Adam's resignation had not been accepted for in the 1883 Minutes he is listed as Chairman with Mr Robert Bourne continuing as the auctioneer. A request was received from the Dartmouth Race Committee for the loan of the telegraph board and numbers. This communication was not met with much enthusiasm by the Committee who refused as it was very likely to get 'out of order'. It was the same year that the death was reported of Mr John Heath, a long-standing member. The receipts for the year were chiefly derived from tolls - £382, entry fees - £103, booths - £76, the total income being £715 against an expenditure of £670. This would also seem to be the year when neighbouring Buckfastleigh Races were established and confirmed by letters received from the secretaries of Buckfastleigh, South Brent and East Cornwall race meetings asking permission for the loan of ropes, flags and bell (the bell had been purchased a few years previously for the sum of ten shillings). As Buckfastleigh was now an established meeting the loan of ropes, etc. was refused. The loan to South Brent was acceded to, on the understanding that if they held a meeting the next year permission would not be renewed. What happened in the case of East Cornwall races is not recorded so I assume the outcome to their request was none too promising. Permissions were sought from landowners/tenants Mr W H Punchard (Bourton Hall) and Messrs Evans and Grills also to place a wicket gate at the Penny Bridge. The private road leading to the racecourse was in need of repair but this request was declined by the owner, Mr Champernowne. Nevertheless a Mr A Cole was employed to 'fill in and repair' by the Committee. This work was to be supervised by the surveyor and Mr A Champernowne. It was suggested that the Duke of Somerset be asked to contribute to the cost.

All landowners and tenants received remuneration for permitting racing across their fields. The trustees of the late Mr Evans applied for an increase in rent to £20. The Committee replied that the rent was raised only a few years ago and wished the trustees to reconsider as they thought that the present payment was sufficient. It was proposed that the Mill Leat be guarded by police and flood gates be affixed to the tramway bridge crossing the leat. Following the Evans' request for an increase in rent in 1884 the next year's meeting provoked a letter from Mr Grills, complaining that his payment was insufficient regarding damage done. He must have had some justification for his claim as a further £2 was paid. The meeting of 1885 produced a loss of £26 which was an unusual occurrence although the profit margins were as low as £5 at times. The Committee undoubtedly kept a tight rein on their spending as one might expect from the business men who were in control. It was the same year that the Committee presented a plain silver tankard to their treasurer, Mr George Mitchell, for his services over fourteen years upon his retirement from office.

In 1883 all tolls were auctioned instead of being let by tender including the Penny Bridge, refreshments, stands and other entertainments. If the bids for the tolls were deemed to be insufficient they were retained by the Race Committee. It is of interest to compare the revenue received through the years from the tolls, e.g. 1861 - £145, 1862 - £156, 1870 - £206, whilst in 1879 they topped the £300 mark, realising £320. In tune with these increases rose the number of police employed. Two of the senior officers were mounted but when one considers the volume of people in attendance the number of thirty-six police in 1879 appears to be very small. The Magistrates Court following the race week did a brisk trade dealing with drunkenness, pickpockets, gambling and riotous behaviour. No doubt as a result of such shenanigans a petition was triggered and signed by 155 Totnes businessmen and presented by Mr Wilson-Cockburn in 1877 to the Magistrates with the request that they do not grant any licence extensions as this would mean more drunkenness and disturbance in the town. The petitioner noted that the races attracted some of the worst elements of society.

In contrast to the seedier side of the races, it was reported by the press in 1882 that Mr Doe of the Salutation Inn, Plymouth, regularly occupied a prime position, his booth being gaily decorated with flowers and with twenty-four waiters being kept fully occupied in waiting on numerous customers. The Band of the South Devon Militia from Plymouth arriving by rail – the railway was pleased to transport the ensemble free of charge – marched through the town entertaining the shoppers and bystanders before making their way to the racecourse.

In 1885 Mr Robert Bourne resigned from the Committee but continued as Auctioneer and in the succeeding year a letter was received from Mr W Mortimer asking for an increase of fifty shillings for the use of his Marsh. It was resolved that as a consequence of the yearly increased demands made by the tenant of the Marsh, the Committee write to the Duke of Somerset asking to be allowed to rent the Marsh and giving the reason for doing so, the present payment being £10. The same year a new Judges' Box was installed and there was an increase in prizemoney of £5 to each of four races (two each day).

A somewhat unusual decision was taken in 1888, due to the time factor involved. The Committee decided to give a donation of £10 to the

Fund raised for the widow and family of the local amateur rider, Mr George Barrett, who had met his death at Totnes Races in 1869, nineteen years previously, and who for so many years as a jockey contributed to the sport at the Totnes race meeting. Further that Mr John C Tucker act as Honorary Secretary to the Fund and that other local race Committees be asked to subscribe; also that cards soliciting subscriptions be placed at hotels in the neighbourhood. I can only assume that the family must have fallen on hard times during the intervening years since his demise and that the need had become more urgent.

The increase in prizemoney in 1886 did not last long, as a reduction of £20 heralded the 1887 meeting, with the races to be advertised in the *Sportsman* and *Sporting Life*. The ensuing year brought a request to obtain an estimate for a plan drawn up by the Surveyor for gates and pillars to be placed at the opening from the Exeter road to the show field on the steeplechase course at Pheasant's Hill. It was decided to pay Mrs Barrett, two sums of £2-10s-0d and that a sum of £100 (total collected) be held at the bank and that she be paid a weekly allowance of ten shillings. The Committee at the time comprised of Mr T C Kellock, Mr A Hingston, Mr G Mitchell, Mr R Nicholls, Mr W H Punchard, Mr J Michelmore, Mr H S Skidmore and Mr W F Tollitt (Surveyor), Mr J C Tucker (Secretary) to which were added Mr F F Hare and Dr J Raby.

Mr Washington Singer offered the sum of £40 to sponsor a Farmers' Race (a Hunter Steeplechase) which was gratefully accepted. A problem had arisen as Mr Punchard of Bourton Hall had not given permission to run over his land. This matter was subsequently resolved.

An application had been received from Sir Thomas Freake and Mr A M Singer to run a match over the 'banking country' and that conditions attached to the resulting approval would be that £5 be deposited with the Stakeholder for damage done and that the Stakes to be run for be deposited in the hands of the Treasurer by 6 p.m. on the evening of the first day of September. The stakes referred to amounted to £25 a side, with the horses concerned named as Baccy and Dandy. It is not recorded as to the outcome of the contest. However, after the racing there was concern expressed as to the amount of broken glass and rubbish left behind by booths and licensed victuallers, shooting galleries and exhibitions. A further problem was that in places the banks of the Mill Leat were breaking down and the flooding which resulted during the succeeding years was to present an on-going thorn in the side of the Race Committee.

At the end of the year the Secretary reported that the Barrett account was nearly drawn so it was resolved that £10 be taken from deposit and placed in the current account as subscriptions to the fund were no longer sufficient to cover the outgoings of ten shillings per week.

The problem with regard to acquiring the necessary permission to run over the land belonging to Mr Punchard resurfaced again in 1889 when a letter of refusal was brought to the notice of the Committee in March. As a result it was decided that the steeplechases, both banking and flying, should, after crossing the river at the Ropewalk, be run on the right hand side of the Exeter road, instead of on both sides as in former years. It had originally been feared that due to Mr Punchard's non co-operation it would not be possible to run the races at all but by redesigning the track it was considered that the new layout was an improvement on the old course. This decision, which showed the determination of the Committee to go ahead come what may, caused a rethink by Mr Punchard who, in July, withdrew his objections. As a result, the Committee rescinded their earlier decision and decided to use the old course of former years. The two-day meeting, however, resulted in a loss of £71 and a surveyor's report indicated that the banks of the Mill Leat were now badly broken away over a considerable distance.

In the following year the death was recorded of Committee member, Mr F Hare, who was replaced by Mr A M Singer. Mr W H Punchard wrote, offering a £40 prize for a race and to put the banks on his land in good order if the Committee would deal with the fences. It was agreed that "all betting men be prohibited from standing on any stools, exhibiting any slates or list, or acting in any way against the Betting Act". Messrs Mortimer Bros were granted copyright for printing racecards and other work at a cost of £13-15s. This meeting also showed a financial loss of £5-9s-7d which at least was an improvement on the previous year.

Mr Jeffrey Michelmore, who had been a long-serving member and was Chairman in 1861, died in 1891. Each Committee member at some time would take his turn in the Chair but Jeffrey Michelmore was one of the stalwarts and an influential presence in the affairs of Totnes Races. He was replaced by Mr P Symons. It was resolved that the banking races be run over the 'old course' described as 'being over the bank' on the hill beyond Bourton Hall, crossing the Exeter road and rounding the head of the quarry. It would seem that this was to be the first occasion that entries were to be closed fourteen days before the fixture. A letter was received from Paignton Race Committee applying for the use of ropes, posts, flags and other plant for their meeting. This was agreed, with the proviso that if their meeting became established this permission would not be extended. As a matter of interest Paignton Race Committee repeated their request the next year for equipment but I hardly think that I need to record the reply. Conditions were amended for a Selling Hunters Steeplechase for half-bred horses over the banking course for forty sovereigns, with the second to receive ten sovereigns: the distance to be 2½ miles.

I have sometimes wondered why the present day point-to-point does not on occasion include a selling race. I understood following investigations with the Jockey Club during the 1970s that there was no reason why this should not be, providing such a 'selling' attachment be made to an existing approved race. However, I was subsequently not able to convince the Committee to which I was Secretary of its merits so that is probably why no one has ever taken it up.

The rift between Mr Punchard and the Committee appeared to have been totally healed as he was invited to join the Stewards Panel for 1891. His demise was to occur just one year later. It was proposed that a temporary bridge be built over the river to include a deviation to the course and to consult with landowners and tenants involved. It was estimated that piers and timber would cost £100. Further discussions were held regarding an admission charge of 6d being levied at the gate, as at other meetings. This proposal was deferred for another year. The condition of the private road leading to the racecourse was still an ongoing problem and a sum of £2 was allocated for its repair. Mr Alfred Michelmore was elected to the Committee, the family name retaining its association with the promotion of the races. A further election to the Committee was Mr H P Skidmore. The Clerk of the Course requested that a new roller be purchased and this was achieved at a cost of five guineas.

Mr John Tucker, the Secretary, resigned in 1895, with Mr W Godfrey appointed in his stead. A new addition to the Committee was Mr Walter J Phillips. Mr W Adams had requested permission to erect a structure at the end of the grandstand for a refreshment stall. This application was denied but to sweeten the pill the Committee agreed to pay him £3 for permitting the public to cross his land to reach the Penny Bridge. The new roller was made available for hire at the cost of two shillings and sixpence per day but in the event of Mr A M Singer requiring its use, then no charge would be made. Permission to use the new road and to cross a bridge to be erected over the Mill Leat from the Great Western Railway was to be obtained; also permission was granted by the rail company for the public to use the track which passes behind the goods shed. The Mill Leat was reported as being dry. The fences opposite the station and at the Tramway Bridge would be broken as in former years to permit access. The Races' finances were by now back in surplus, albeit by only a small amount, and it was decided that Messrs Punchard Jr. and Barter be not charged for the use of the roller when rolling the land run over during the Races.

Agricultural shows on the racecourse had been granted dispensation to continue but the Committee had received an unusual letter, by today's standards, from Mr Washington Singer who expressed the wish that his name be omitted from the Stewards Panel, until he had received a list of officials for his approval! Without batting an eyelid the Committee forthwith complied with his request, so such behaviour must have been accepted as normal at the time.

An amendment was proposed to the race programme in 1895 which would permit professional jockeys to ride in the hunt steeplechase and that colours instead of hunting dress be worn. Concern was expressed that the Mill Leat remained dry. It was initially thought that, if agreed by Totnes Town Council, a one inch pipe fitted to the water main would be the best method of filling the water jump but after further deliberation it was decided that enquiries be made as to whether water could be supplied from the Upper Dart to fill the leat to protect the grandstand (possibly to deal with the fire risk) and to supply the water jump.

In 1896 a report was received by the Committee with regard to damage to the Marsh caused by contractors' wagons going 'to and fro' to the weir. Other business included that the owners of the mill property be asked to allow the fenders at the head of the leat to be lowered each day after the last race, so as to lessen the quantity of water in the leat (a case of one extreme to the other). The Surveyor also recommended that the bed of the River Dart, where the horses crossed, be repaired. It was also agreed to rent the stable at the back of No. 3 Fore Street to board the long-distance equine traveller at a yearly rental of £4. This appeared to be a straight swap, as notice to quit was given on Mr Phillips' stable. A request was to hand, from Mr Robert A D Fleming of Bigadon, seeking permission to erect a tent in the grandstand enclosure for the purpose of entertaining a few friends to lunch. This matter was referred to the lessee of spaces on the course. Three owners, Messrs Joe Hamlyn, H S Johnson and E Wand wrote asking for an abatement in their entry and weighing fees for the 1896 meeting. However, it was decided that no exception could be given.George Bulteel sponsored the Maiden Steeplechase in the sum of 40 sovereigns. This too was one of many years when the racecourse benefited from the sale of the winner of the 'seller' to the tune of £18 as the horse Bazaar entered to be sold for £50, realised £86. A very successful season resulted in a profit of £133-3s-5d.

1897 proved a more dramatic year. Firstly, Mr A M Singer resigned from the Committee and as a sponsor. This was capped by the communication from Mr Washington Singer who enclosed a cheque for £10. He wrote, "If I had not promised, I should not have subscribed anything and will not do so in future. Despite being a good supporter in the past, both as a subscriber and bringing horses to run, I am surprised at the scant courtesy I have received at the hands of your Committee." A reply was sent saying how sorry they were that Mr Singer felt aggrieved and to enquire as to what the discourtesy might be and by whom. I have to leave the matter in suspension as I am unable to find any further correspondence as to what the final outcome was to be. The Races must have been a great success as the press report states that, "Today we saw the most popular racing fixture of the West, known as the Derby of the West, from the fact that it still retains the unique distinction of remaining the only meeting of any importance held under National Hunt rules which admits the public without charge to the course, except of course Epsom Downs."

This year, in view of complaints which reached them, the Committee decided to veto the established custom of allowing roundabouts, shooting galleries and similar paraphernalia to occupy the space between the course and the grandstands. Consequently there was a full view of the racing from the stands with only a dozen or so refreshment booths and a score of refreshment and sweet stalls taking up their positions on the ground. As an experiment for clearing the course for the benefit of the occupants of the stands the idea worked admirably but considerable disappointment was expressed, especially by those attending from the country, that the time-honoured appearance of the Marsh had been so altered and that their amusements had disappeared. The press reported that they spent their time between events in listening to the charms of the phonograph, buying from and being sold to by 'the auctioneers' who plied a vigorous trade, a lady doing good business or in watching the expert feats of itinerant performers many of whom reaped a rich harvest of pence. Musicians of various types – 'black and white' - also kept them cheerful with their ditties, the inveterate 'Adolphus' who takes nothing but silver appearing more than usually cheeky.

The report concluded with the statement that the entire absence of amusements on the course and in the town made the first day a record for quietness, the majority of the people going home immediately the racing was over. The press also commented that the attendance on the second day, for the general public, was far in advance of the first day, it being estimated that quite 12,000 people crowded the course and lined the ropes, while vehicles were very numerous. A bandstand was located opposite the grandstands which, as well as the paddock and offices, were built by Mr John Richardson of Totnes who had been lessee, with few exceptions, for the past twenty years. This year he paid the Committee £439 for the tolls and it must have been gratifying for him to find his enterprise repaid by the liberal patronage accorded in the stands which were full to overflowing with the élite of the district, while the paddock was comfortably filled before each race by judges of horseflesh – good and otherwise.

In 1898 the two banking races were converted to fly fences and the course builders were listed as Messrs B and H Veale, F Cole and W Timewell. The following year prizemoney returned to its former level of £50 of which the second horse received £10. Capt. Bainbridge wrote complaining that the entrances to the grandstand were insufficient. It was agreed that alterations should be made. Seven hundred and forty bundles of birch would be required for course building and purchased from John Heath at a cost of eight guineas.

A donation of five pounds was the first recorded payment to the Cottage Hospital, which provided a good service to the racecourse.

At the turn of the century seating to accommodate two hundred people was installed in the grandstand in two rows. The price of admission to the stand was increased from four shillings to five shillings. The paddock was extended, for which the admittance fee was to be raised to half-a-crown. A new set of scales was purchased at a cost of £9-5s-0d, and the receipts from the tolls now topped the five hundred pounds mark being returned at £520. Two steeplechases were to carry extra prizemoney being increased by ten pounds each to £60. The Committee agreed to a suggestion made to them by Mr Robert Harvey that a space be railed off for the carriages of the Stewards and Committee. It is to be noted that Mr Washington Singer was invited to be a member of the Stewards Panel so perhaps hatchets had been buried. A fee of ten shillings was paid to the fishermen for helping to remove the carcase of Ballyshannon who had met with a fatal accident and had rolled into the river.

An internal matter dominated the early part of 1901 when the Secretary, Mr W Godfrey Jnr. was asked to resign, as not having attended to his duties and to hand over all books and papers and other property of the Committee within one week. The post was subsequently advertised and brought three applications, the outcome of which was that Mr W J Hayman was appointed at a salary of £10. A letter was despatched to Mr R E Bourne (Auctioneer) to ensure his prompt attendance in the paddock immediately after the finish of each selling race to prevent unnecessary delay. For such a directive to be made tells its own story of the lax state of affairs which must have prevailed. A letter had been received from Admiral Parker claiming that he had been refused a free pass over the Penny Bridge. The Committee offered their apologies and very much regretted that he had been embarrassed. Mr J Blake wrote asking for the second prize of £3 won by his horse, Boa, to be paid. The Committee replied that the owner had received three letters requesting a fee of £1 which was outstanding to be paid to them. They also pointed out that a disqualified horse is not entitled to any prizemoney and that unless fees were paid his name would be sent for inclusion on the forfeit list.

Mr Leigh Densham joined the Committee in 1902, the year that it was decided to construct a bridge from the back of the grandstand passing over the Buckfastleigh railway line. Local owner, Mr J Hamlyn, requested permission to offer several horses for sale on the course at the next meeting. The Secretary was instructed to write and inform him that it was not to be a collective sale but that the horses might be offered after the race in which they had run. Private detectives were hired for duty at the races for which two, Messrs Godden and Marlow, were ex-police inspectors from London, their fee being five guineas each for the two days. This was in all probability as a consequence of events which had occurred twelve months before when the

Totnes Times reported,

"The wins scored by three favourites in succession hit some of the bookmakers hard and a couple bolted from the ring and were endeavouring to make themselves scarce 'ere their patrons sought fulfilment of their obligations from them. Police Sergeants Webber, Yendell and Pratt figured prominently and the police won, the defaulters being marched back and although full of excuses they were compelled by various threats to pay over but they were unable to do this until they had borrowed sufficient from obliging friends."

In 1903 the Clerk of the Course informed the Committee that Dr Johnson had been using the race marsh as a training ground for his horses and that the tenant Mr Evans had given his consent. Letters were sent to both gentlemen pointing out the damage which was being done to the course. It was decided to increase the number of races to be run each day, from five to six, and that the charges for the Penny Bridge should rise from one penny to sixpence for each crossing; also that two turnstiles be provided. It was logical that, with the demise of the Penny Bridge it was in future referred to as the 'Sixpenny Bridge'. A letter from Mr Strode pointed out that the grandstand had been badly constructed. It was resolved that the present four tiers of seating be increased to seven and that they be made windproof and watertight; also that there be a Ladies entrance.

It was brought to the Committee's notice that part of the race marsh amounting to just over four acres was to be sold by public auction on behalf of Mrs Champernowne. A sub-committee was formed to attend the sale with a mandate to purchase if at all possible. This was achieved for the sum of £600. The tenant, Mrs Petersen, was subsequently given notice to quit. The Committee also rented a new store to be converted into stabling. The four ground rents paid for the year were to the Duke of Somerset, Mr M Evans, Mr J Wood and Mrs Petersen. In addition to the usual donation to the Cottage Hospital, the Totnes Nursing Association was also a beneficiary.

The next year (1904) saw the death of the Secretary, Mr W J Hayman and the appointment of his successor, Mr W H Nugent. Problems had arisen with regard to the river crossing near the Ropewalk and it was agreed that forty loads of stone be deposited on the river bed. The weather had been so bad the previous year, the meeting being buffeted by such high winds that several bookmakers' stands were blown over. Another victim of the gales was a large marquee which was sheltering numerous persons, "Nobody was hurt but everybody was wet". Following the purchase of a part of the marsh some successful 'horse trading' was conducted with Mr C W Tayleur who owned Broadmarsh, which amounted to just over eleven acres. It was agreed that Mr Tayleur be paid £15 for the right to run over his marsh and that he in turn would pay the races £10 for renting their land with the Committee reserving the right to race over it. The meeting resulted in a loss of £44-17s-4d.

1905 brought a new appointment to the Committee with the election of Mr C J Swears. They were to receive something of a shock to the system when in receipt of a letter from Messrs Weatherby stating that the practice of farming out the receipts for the grandstand must cease as local stewards must have cognisance of all matters connected to the meeting together with all tolls. Furthermore the programme should contain an Open race each day to the value of 100 sovereigns with no reduction to other prizes. Correspondence with Messrs Weatherby brought about a dispensation with regard to the increase in prizemoney with the implementation of this directive being postponed due to the races having sustained a loss the previous year. The death was reported of the long-serving Committee member, Mr R V Nicholls, who also acted as Treasurer. Mr R E Bourne was elected in his place. Mr W F Telfer was installed as the new Treasurer. The death also occurred of Admiral Parker a well known and respected Steward at the races.

Flooding was an issue on the course due to the choking of a gutter on the marsh in the occupation of Mr Furneaux. It was proposed to install a nine inch pipe to be laid alongside the present gutter. In view of the losses incurred the previous year it was decided that the Secretary and Mr Heath be asked to canvas the town for subscriptions to the Race Fund. Following the Races the accounts showed that five owners were in arrears for their entry fees. One owner complained of an overcharge for stabling at the Town Arms Hotel. A small profit for the year amounted to £6-17s-9½d. Items from the balance sheet showed expenditure for the purchase of twelve flags for decoration, also bunting for the front of the grandstand, whilst Messrs R Drennan and W H Frost were paid £1-6s-4d and 18s-8d for advertising, with printing costs at £10-10s-3d and Messrs Mortimer Bros. £2-12s-0d. Receipts listed included gate money, admission to stands and paddock £610-6s-3d, carriage enclosure £33-12s-0d. Mr William Frost was to become a proprietor of the *Totnes Times* in future years. The course had now become subject to inspection by a representative of the National Hunt Committee.

1906 heralded the end of free entry to the course. It was decided to levy an admission charge of 6d at all entrances – bridge usage to be extra at 1 shilling. Turnstiles were to be purchased at £9 each. Two mounted constables were engaged to patrol the course in addition to the usual complement of police and that four Committee members act as finance stewards, "to pay special attention to the men employed at the turnstiles and the change office". The first handicapper not to be a Committee member was Mr L'Anson whose remuneration was based on 2s-6d per entry with a 5 shillings addition for all starters. It was resolved that no one be allowed to land on the course from the boat, which had frequently been provided to take the public across the river. It was agreed that brewery wagons be charged £1-1s-0d for coming on the course.

Subsequent to the meeting a complaint was received from owners regarding the handicapper – nothing has changed in this respect up to the present day, however the outcome was that a Mr Ward would be approached for next year's races. The cost of erecting the stands was £254 which conveniently leads on to 1907 when discussions were taking place in respect of building at least one permanent grandstand with consideration given to a similar second stand. Estimates from Messrs David Rowell & Co. - £513 for stand, ironwork and corrugated roof – and Messrs Kinsman Bros. - £500 for woodwork and concrete – were accepted. The main grandstand was to measure 150 feet in length to cater for 700 spectators and to include a bar and pavilion in the rear. It was to be sited on the higher turn of the course where it would command a magnificent view of the track and the further fields over which racing took place. The contractors estimated a timescale of eight weeks to complete. It was decided to erect the second stand on the Committee's own ground, below the main grandstand. This smaller edition was to measure eighty feet in length and to be positioned ten feet from the rails. An unclimbable fence was to be erected, 500 feet in length, between the two stands, with a nine feet opening for a gate. Two pay boxes were to be situated at the second stand with an extra pay box at the bridge entrance of the main grandstand. A refreshment bar comprising two lengths of forty-five feet each would be sited at the side of the paddock. Admission charges were to be: one-horse conveyance 5 shillings, plus 6d per occupant; two-horse conveyance 10 shillings, three- or four-horse conveyance £1. Further changes were to be made the next year (1908).

Three bridges were erected in front of the grandstand spanning the leat to improve the access for spectators. A toll bridge was built crossing the leat by which the public gained entry from the railway station and for the first time motor cars would be allowed on the course at a fee of 10 shillings per car plus 6d per occupant. The bridges across the leat to the grandstand, the bridge to the second stand and the Sixpenny Bridge had to date been only of a temporary nature, being erected and taken down on a yearly basis. It was now decided that permanent structures should be put in place. Application was also made to the Post Office for a telegraphic communication to be installed at the course.

During the year, the Secretary, Mr W H Nugent, resigned due to poor health. The position was advertised in the local press which brought eight applications, the appointee being Mr J Mason. Mr G Mitchell had declined to act as Judge so for the first time it was decided to appoint a professional, which resulted in Mr A E Hancock being engaged at a fee of ten guineas for the meeting. These were to be the early days of the Hancock family's association as judges for horseracing which was to last up to the latter years of the twentieth century with the retirement of the Senior Jockey Club Judge, Mr Michael Hancock.

The Women's Temperance Association applied for, and was granted, a stand and the Secretary was instructed to arrange with a chemist for a supply of bandages, lint, etc. for use in the case of accidents, on condition that only the material used was to be charged for! Races that attracted only a small number of entries were re-opened, a ruling which has in recent years been re-introduced to present day racing. Very little of note transpired in the Committee room during 1909 except that a donation of three guineas was given to the Mayoress's Fund for the purpose of purchasing a wheeled ambulance subject to the vehicle being placed at the disposal of the Race Committee on each day, the Mayoress agreeing to these terms. A horse ambulance was already in use.

Prizemoney was raised by £40 for each day's racing in 1910 together with the purchase of number cloths. After discussion it was decided to share the cost and usage of the cloths with Plymouth Races who would have first use and return them laundered and in good condition. Twenty-five sets numbered 1-20 were acquired for the sum of £15. The Committee accepted the resignation of Mr W J Phillips and following the death of Dr Johnson as racecourse medical officer, Dr Stanley C Jellicoe was appointed to fill the vacancy.

A long dry spell prior to racing in 1911 saw the Fire Brigade employed to water the hard portions of the course on the afternoon preceding the first day's action, to include the landing side of jumps. An unfortunate event occurred subsequent to the fixture when the Clerk of the Course, Mr Richard Heath, incurred a fine of five pounds by the National Hunt Committee on account of the Open Ditch not being of the proper dimensions, whilst in 1912 the death was reported of Mr C W Tayleur, a long time patron of the Races. Twenty garden seats were purchased for the grandstand enclosure at a cost of 19 shillings each and some forty bookmakers were in attendance although not more than six were permitted in front of the grandstand. A meeting was arranged to take place at Plymouth to discuss bookmakers, with Capt. A Daniel (Plymouth Races) in the Chair. Plymouth was also represented by Messrs W Derry, C Spooner and A Godfrey with R Vicary (Newton Abbot), Messrs G Mitchell and C J Swears (Totnes) and Mr J Wakeham (South Brent). Apologies were received from the representatives of Exeter, Buckfastleigh and Torquay. Topics for discussion were not confined to the bookmaking fraternity – for whom charges for admission were agreed – but that a letter representing the whole of the race committees on the Devonshire circuit be sent to Messrs Weatherby to try to prevent a further increase in stakemoney, as suggested by the National Hunt Committee. Mr R E Bourne tendered his resignation from the Committee and was replaced by Mr Charles Barran.

It was the end of an era for the Heath family in 1913 when the death occurred of Mr Richard Heath whose family had occupied the position of Clerk of the Course since the very early days of racing at Totnes and whose career has already been noted. The new appointment of Mr C H Barran was to be for the duration of the year. However, there was to be a sting in the tail for the appointee as the National Hunt Committee refused to grant him a Clerk's licence – I wonder if this was because he was a member of the Race Committee? As there were two other applicants for the position it was decided to approach Mr H W Pye who accepted the post.

A fire claim, on insurance, was made in respect of a blaze which originated in an area underneath the main grandstand, this space having been used for storage purposes. It was thought at the time that the cause was arson due to suffragettes. Perhaps a young lad with a box of matches may have been a more realistic alternative. It was decided to award the contract for building the second stand to Mr T E Brook, its permanency having been put on hold. The *Western Morning News* was asked to publish a full list of entries as was done in the *Western Daily Mercury* and that no races would be run across the river this year. This was to be the final race meeting to be held before the First World War.

The Committee received a request in 1914 from the Aeroplane Committee in connection with their demonstration at the Devon County Show, for permission to use the grandstand. At a Committee meeting held on 8th August a discussion was held with regard to altering the track at both the higher and lower ends plus the construction of a permanent weighing room and offices but due to the very grave crisis in world affairs which was looming it was agreed that application to the National Hunt Committee be made for the abandonment of the Races fixed for 9th and 10th September.

It is not possible to read the Minutes of that Committee meeting without a sense of foreboding due to the horrific events, carnage and sacrifice which was about to befall the country during the next four years and which could not have been fully envisaged by the writer at the time.

The first flight of hurdles in the home straight
Photo courtesy of Totnes Image Bank & Rural Archive

Runners between obstacles
Photo courtesy of Totnes Image Bank & Rural Archive

*A close up view of horses negotiating a hurdle: compare construction to
present day version*
Photo courtesy of Totnes Image Bank & Rural Archive

*Blue Pencil (J Vowles) races neck and neck with Ma-Chin-On (C Spares)
before dead-heating in the 2 mile Selling Hurdle, 1938*
Photo courtesy of Totnes Image Bank & Rural Archive

Runners rounding the bend after the winning post. Note the pronounced lean to the right of the horses, with cars close to the running rail

Photo courtesy of Totnes Image Bank & Rural Archive

Totnes & Bridgetown
RACES

(Under National Hunt Rules).

Second Day.   THURSDAY, **SEPT. 1st, 1938.**   **Price 6d.**

PATRONS :

The Duke of Somerset; Lord Mamhead; The Lord Mildmay of Flete; Sir Alfred Goodson, Bart.; Commdr. C. H. Davey, R.N., O.B.E., M.F.H.

STEWARDS :

Major Sir Samuel E. Harvey; H. F. Brunskill, Esq.; Major F. H. B. Passy; G. H. Turner, Esq.

DIRECTORS :

Capt. F. J. C. Holdsworth (Chairman), Lt.-Col. F. K. Windeatt, Mr. A. Hingston, Mr. W. R. Holman, Capt. H. B. Kauntze, Mr. J. G. Kellock, Mr. G. F. B. Marks and Major W. G. Loveys.

OFFICIALS :

Lt.-Col. S. Findlay, Handicapper; Mr. J. Wakeham, Hon. Starter and Auctioneer; Mr. A. E. Hancock, Judge; Mr. H. L. Crockwell, Clerk of the Scales; Dr. Stanley C. Jellicoe, Hon. Surgeon; Capt. H. B. Kauntze, M.R.C.V.S., Hon. Veterinary Surgeon; Mr. J. Mason, Secretary; Lt.-Col. F. K. Windeatt, Stakeholder, Elmfield, Totnes; Mr. T. H. Wilton Pye, Clerk of the Course.

NOTICE.—Owners and Trainers are requested to apply for their Admission Tickets to the Course, etc., to Mr. T. H. Wilton Pye, at the Royal Seven Stars Hotel, on each morning of the Races from 11 a.m. to 12.30 p.m.

Steeplechase Course, leave Red Flag on the Right.

The Water will only be jumped twice in Two Miles and three times in Three Miles.

In all Steeplechases, the last time round, Horses will take the Hurdle Course to finish.

Racecard cover of the last day's racing at Totnes, 1st September 1938

The Old Grandstand converted into a store, 1985. No longer in existence.

Part of the stable block in 1985, now long gone.

CHAPTER 8
THE WAR YEARS AND THE RESUMPTION
OF RACING TO 1939

During the period of the First World War the Committee continued to meet with a view to maintaining the course and their equipment. Birch that was stored at Bourton Hall was sold but all other fixtures and fittings were repaired, painted and, where necessary, treated with solignum to act as a preservative so that all would be in order for the resumption of racing in 1919. Prior to the September fixture an application was received from the Totnes Agricultural Show Committee for the use of the grandstand and other equipment for their summer exhibition. At an early Race Committee meeting it was decided to increase the price of admission. Entrance to course, stand and paddock was agreed at: back entrance 6s-6d, course entrance 5s-6d, paddock 3 shillings, entrance to course only 1 shilling, motor vehicles capable of seating ten £3, with a 12 shillings charge for occupants of motor cars and carriages. However, at a subsequent meeting two months later it was agreed that some of these charges should be further increased in the light of Entertainment Tax becoming payable: the back entrance to the grandstand rising to 10 shillings, the second stand 8 shillings, the paddock 3 shillings and the course 2 shillings A visiting Course Inspector, Mr Peel (of whom we shall hear more in future years) was appointed by the National Hunt Committee and a directive was in operation that only six Stewards might serve on the Panel. To add to the festivities the Town Council had let space on The Plains for the whole of Race Week to Messrs Hancock, for their fairground, and in consequence a concert which had been arranged to take place on Vire Island was cancelled due to the impracticability of competing with the noise and activities on The Plains, just a stone's throw away. The race meeting proved a great success with crowds flocking back with the result that H.M. Customs and Excise benefited to the extent of £367-15s-10d in Entertainment Tax.

It was learned that Newton Abbot Races had been granted a fixture date in 1920 for Tuesday, 7th September, the day before the usual first day's racing at Totnes. A letter was sent to the National Hunt Committee pointing out the close proximity and the injustice which would be done, forcing Totnes to apply for Friday and Saturday, 10th and 11th September. Further complications had arisen due to the Course Inspector's report (Mr Peel) that considerable work was required to put the course in order and to the water jump, otherwise no fixture would be granted for next year. It was agreed that a farmer be asked as to what his terms might be to supply a team of horses and harrows for use on the racecourse, to remove 'hummocks', etc. after which three or four men would be employed to fill in the holes. Nevertheless, in the spring of 1920 the condition of the race marsh was still presenting problems and a meeting on the course with the Course Inspector was arranged. It was decided to purchase a Cambridge roller and that the work be put in hand. Permission was given to the Totnes Agricultural Show Committee for their continued use of the grandstand and the ground but that their request for the use of the water jump be refused. The charge for the use of the stand would be £75, owing to the heavy expense incurred annually on its maintenance. As a footnote, the Totnes Show reported very good entries for the year of 140 horses, 50 cattle and 60 sheep.

Two new faces joined the Committee, Lt. Col. F K Windeatt and Mr Alfred Hingston, whilst Mr John Wakeham was appointed as Starter, a role that he was to occupy for the remaining years in the life of Totnes Races, until its closure in 1938. Since racing had resumed after the War, new patrons' names were listed on the racecard including Sir Alfred Goodson, Sir R Newman, M.P., Col. C R Burn, M.P., Lt. Col. C Williams, M.P., Com. C H Davey, O.B.E., M.F.H., and Mr Oxley Durant Parker, whilst successive Dukes of Somerset were regular supporters. Col. Garratt, a long standing member of the Stewards Panel had died and Mr Joe Hamlyn replaced him. For the forthcoming meeting it was agreed that a silver cup to the value of 20 sovereigns be awarded to the winning rider in the South Devon Amateur Riders' Open Hunter Steeplechase and to use the subscriptions of £12-7s-0d, already collected, to this end. Mr George Mitchell agreed to make up the balance required. An application was made to the Town Council for a supply of water to be laid on to the grandstand on the two race days. The Council replied that the charge would be five pounds. The Committee thought this to be excessive in consideration that the Agricultural Show Committee received the supply free of charge so decided to offer two pounds. In order to smarten up the appearance of the course the construction known as the Golf House was demolished and the site levelled in preparation for the building of permanent offices and a new Golf House.

1920 was also the year that reference is first made to the employment of the St John's Ambulance Brigade. Mr Bulley was to become the fence builder with birch for the fences purchased at 2s-3d per bundle delivered; also that a canvas screen be attached to the leat side of the paddock to prevent people overlooking. Three further items of note at the end of the year were the resignation of Mr Leigh Densham as a member; that next year's stake money would top £900 and that the Secretary's salary be increased to £40.

The New Year brought an offer made by Mr Charles S Morris of the Seven Stars Hotel that he was prepared to sell part of Broadmarsh to the Race Committee if they were interested. A sub-committee was formed to look into the matter and arrange a meeting with Mr Morris. A satisfactory outcome was achieved with the Committee being able to complete the purchase. Three tenders had been received for the erection of the permanent buildings in the paddock from Messrs W J Goodridge, W Reeves & Sons and T E Brook, all being local tradesmen from Totnes. Mr Brook's tender of £303-15s-0d, being the lowest, was accepted. Negotiations were entered into with both Plymouth Races and Buckfastleigh Races with a view to sharing saddle cloths (number cloths) at each racecourse, Totnes contributing half the cost. This was found to be acceptable to all parties.

It was thought that Police Constable Philpott should be engaged for two nights prior to racing to prevent boys from entering the grandstand and to avoid vandalism. Other recommendations were that owners, trainers, jockeys and officials should have refreshments provided in the Committee Room and that free stabling be available to owners from 12 noon on the day before racing to a similar time the day after its conclusion.

The Committee approached the Great Western Railway with an offer to purchase the piece of land which they leased on an annual basis. The Railway Company replied, inviting an offer which, when duly made, sealed the deal for £150 to add to the Weir field property which had been acquired earlier in the year. More work on the course was proposed, firstly that a permanent bridge over the Mill Leat leading to the grandstand and paddock be constructed and then, following a meeting with Mr Peel, the Course Inspector, it was thought to be beneficial to extend the present 'dressing room' and weighing room by 15 feet towards the grandstand, with the entrance door at the end of the building and grandstand enclosure, the work to be carried out by Messrs T E Brook. A batten was also deemed necessary to be placed at the end of the bridge to prevent injury to horses and jockeys through members of the public crossing over the course. The space under the higher end of the grandstand would be converted into a tea room, whilst the sale ring needed levelling. Mr John Wakeham, the Starter, was appointed as Auctioneer for the two days at a fee of five guineas, now undertaking the dual role. Refreshments were to be provided for Stewards, owners, trainers and officials but with the directive that the number of bottles of whisky should not exceed six per day!

A request from Rev. A H Sayers for boys to come on to the course to distribute bills in connection with a concert to be held at the Seymour Hotel was granted, provided that they paid their admission charge. The Town Council asked for the use of the horse roller owned by the Committee which was agreed. However the opportunity afforded was seized upon as the letter of consent also pointed out the excessive charge that was being levied for the use of the water supply to the grandstand, in the hope that a reduction be made. It would appear that the Town Council took scant notice of this request for when they again applied for the use of the roller two years later the Committee repeated their plea for a substantial reduction in the charge for the use of the Town water on race days.

In 1923 three additional members joined the Committee, Capt. F J C

Holdsworth, Mr Hamilton Coffey and Mr James D Manley. Mr Coffey's involvement was to be brief as he resigned after just one year. The Course Inspector reported that extra railings were required at the lower end of the course on the hurdle track; that after racing the open ditch should not be filled in but fenced around with iron hurdles, also the water jump in a similar fashion.

The Totnes Agricultural Show continued to use the course and stands for their Annual Show for which they paid a fee of £75. In 1924 they sought a reduction and sent a deputation to plead their case. The Committee were unable to see their way to accede to the request but agreed to give a donation of £20 in lieu. The Golf Club successfully applied for permission to place a green and tee on the grandstand enclosure and it was decided to erect a new number board to be fixed on a raised concrete plinth forty feet from the rails and between the Leat and the fence in the enclosure. The amount of litter that was left behind after racing was increasing, with bottles, glass and paper becoming an eyesore and a nuisance.

In 1925 the Committee received a letter from Messrs A Michelmore & Son on behalf of the Duke of Somerset offering to sell the lower part of Broadmarsh. After deliberation it was agreed that an offer of £1,200 be made for the land in question. This was accepted as a fair price by the vendor and the transfer completed. The same year heralded the erection of permanent buildings to house the turnstiles with the work once again being undertaken by Messrs T E Brook. To assist with the promotion and advertising of the races it was decided to place a notice board in Little Marsh, near the Totnes Bridge, on which would be displayed the dates of forthcoming meetings. It was thought that there was likely to be a shortage of overnight stabling for horses with the result that the Surveyor and Secretary arranged an interview with Sir Robert Harvey of Dundridge, Harberton, and Mr Trist of Tristford House, Harberton, with a request for the possible use of their stables at Bowden, Totnes, and Tristford if required. Four names were put forward for consideration as new members of the Committee: Sir D Twomey, Capt. Goldsmith, Mr Alfred Hingston and Mr William R Holman, the last two being appointed.

By 1927 it was reported that improvements were needed at the higher end of the course, especially to the top turn. In addition it was learned that lead weights would have to be provided for the jockeys at future race meetings. (Did they provide their own in former years?) It was resolved to approach the Buckfastleigh Race Committee as to whether they would be prepared to pay half the cost of a set of weights which could be used by both Committees on the same principle that the saddle cloths were shared. It was agreed that the Totnes Race Committee should become a member of the Racecourse Association and to be represented at their meetings. Consideration was also given to the Committee's liability for National Health Insurance Stamps in relation to the duties of the Secretary.

The death occurred of Committee member Mr C J Swears of Puddavine House, a valued member and long time supporter of the races. A communication was received from Mr A Bucknell of Bagborough, Taunton, the owner of Landman entered in the South Devon Steeplechase stating that his horse had died on 15th August and requesting that he may be excused payment of the entry money. This was agreed.

As a result of enquiries made with regard to additional overnight stabling Mr Narramore approached the Committee offering the availability of five boxes, subject to agreeing the terms of 5 shillings per box per day, plus part of the cost of putting them in order. It was decided to settle the matter with a single payment of £2.

A letter was dispatched to the Racecourse Association in 1928 with regard to a practice which had become prevalent, for horses entered in races and present in the paddock and apparently capable of running, being withdrawn by the owners or trainers. An approach from Totnes Golf Club requesting financial assistance was considered with the outcome being that a £20 donation was made. Further discussion took place in respect of the question of building extra horse boxes at the lower end of the paddock and the erection and operation of a Totalisator in the grandstand enclosure.

A momentous decision made in 1928 was the dissolution of the Committee in favour of forming a Company with a Board of Directors with limited guarantee. The first Board consisted of Mr George Mitchell (Chairman), Mr A Michelmore, Mr C Barran, Mr T Maye, Mr J. D Manley, Capt. F J C Holdsworth and Lt. Col. F K Windeatt, with Mr J Mason as Secretary. The registered office was 59 Fore Street, Totnes. Mr W F Tollitt, Mr A Hingston and Mr W R Holman were invited to join the following year bringing the number up to the full complement of ten.

The next decade was to see several changes to the Board commencing with the death of Mr Charles Barran in 1929; the following year brought the retirement of Mr J D Manley and in 1932, Mr William Tollitt passed away. A spate of new appointments followed: Mr Donald M Petherick (1932), Mr J G Kellock (1933), Capt. H B Kauntze (1933) and Mr G B Marks (1934).

The Directors carried on the good work in improving facilities on the course, which had been a priority for the now defunct Committee. In 1931 the number of on-course boxes was more than doubled being increased from sixteen to thirty-six with, in addition, the erection of a new unsaddling enclosure.

The death of Mr George Mitchell who had been elected as Chairman of the initial Board following its formation in 1928 was announced in April 1934, his replacement being Mr G B Marks. In recognition of his contribution to the Company and the racecourse it was decided that a race be named in his honour on the second day of that year's meeting, the selected event being the restyled "Mitchell Memorial Handicap Hurdle", to be run over two miles.

Further losses to the Company were to occur 1935 and 1938 with the passing of Thomas Maye and Alfred Michelmore, both of whom were founder appointees to the Board.

Starter, Augustus Hingston, circa 1900

1950 Company Dinner at the Royal Seven Stars Hotel, Capt. F J C Holdsworth (centre) handing silver cups for competition at Newton Abbot and Buckfastleigh Races to Mr C L Vicary (left) and Mr R Hoare (right)

1971 Company Dinner at Chateau Bellevue Hotel. Race cups being handed to Mr A C Bulpin (left) and Brig. Sir Ralph Rayner, M.P., for competition at Newton Abbot and Devon & Exeter Races by Mr J G Kellock

1960 Company Dinner at Chateau Bellevue Hotel

Company Dinner at Holne Chase Hotel, Ashburton, 1978

1963. Mr J G Kellock presenting a silver salver to Mr R A Bloomfield, rider of Grand Morn II, winner of the Totnes Open Hunter Steeplechase, Newton Abbot. Holding the horse is owner Mr G H Shepheard

1964. Mr A C Bulpin presenting a silver salver to Mr I S G Lang, winner of the Totnes Open Hunter Steeplechase, Newton Abbot, with rider Mr M A Capps. Trainer S Kernick is on the left

Mr B L Toll presenting a silver salver to Mr T C Widdicombe owner of Weensland Lad, winner of the Totnes Open Hunter Steeplechase, Newton Abbot, with rider Mr A Flood, 1961

Mr A C Bulpin presenting a silver salver to Mrs S Knipe owner of Buchan Loon winner of Totnes Open Hunter Steeplechase, Newton Abbot, 1968

Mr J G Kellock presenting a silver salver to Mr A E Hill, owner of French Flag, winner of the Totnes Open Hunter Steeplechase, Newton Abbot 1972

CHAPTER 9
UP AND RUNNING – RACING BETWEEN THE WARS

After an interval of four years without the sport, the general public were only too eager to welcome the return of horse racing to these shores (racing having continued in Ireland) in the attempt to pick up the threads and to revive a popular pastime. The racehorse population had been drastically reduced due to the pensioning off of many animals which were in their prime at the outbreak of war, whilst others had met a more grisly fate. The studs were only operating at a low level and private owners and farmers who had kept a couple of broodmares for the production of the thoroughbred were now more interested in the heavier breeds for working the farm, to replace those animals which had been requisitioned by the army. It therefore came as no surprise when, in 1919, the number of horses in training showed a significant reduction. Nevertheless the entry for Totnes and Bridgetown was considered to be satisfactory in the circumstances.

Local jockey Bobby Gordon celebrated his return to the course with a victory aboard Mr L Lysaght's The Fly III, in the Somerset Handicap Steeplechase carrying the steadier of 12st. 13lb. on the opening day, the combination supplementing their gains with a 'walkover' the next day, when although handicapped at only 1lb. less, no one was prepared to take him on. Some 200-300 cars were parked on the course with three rows lining the finishing straight

. Not everyone was enamoured about racing being restricted to Broadmarsh, some still pining for the river crossing and the old track which had climbed the hill to Mock Wood. A letter was received from Major Longworth, a well known owner/rider before the War, addressed to Mr R M Bourne and the Committee. He wrote,

"I was very pleased to come to Totnes Races again, after missing them for so many years. But what can you be thinking of, to do away with the old hill and river course? The meeting without that is nothing more than a 'flapping show' and I doubt if the National Hunt Committee will renew your licence for such a course. In the old course you had something unique – there was no other in England like it and it was famous far and wide. It required some horsemanship and judgement to win there, which is not called for in the same way in galloping round and round over an ordinary course. It is also a race worth people's while to come and see. Your Committee should use that course again and should go back to the old days and cross the river twice. You used always to attract plenty of runners (not so in later years – Ed.) and you would get a different class of horse and owner – a class of horse which, when the entries have been made, are more likely to be run than the ordinary moderate 'chaser or hurdler which is entered on chance and not run unless he has a good chance of winning. For heaven's sake, encourage the owner/rider who comes for the sport of the thing. Use some imagination in framing the conditions and attract the horse that has been regularly hunted and the soldier's horse. If your Committee has plenty of money, you ought to be able to make up some good races each day for that class of horse and I would suggest doing all in your power to attract runners in all of your races, either by rebating the entrance fee to the horses that actually start or even (if you are very rich) of requiring a fee at all or by giving an owner a 'bit towards expenses'. It will come to that in time, if racing is to go on, in view of the enormously increased expense. The public appear to have plenty of money and there is no difficulty in filling the stand. The old course should be used again if the meeting is to go on. What a shame when you have got a really historic course like that, to lightly abandon it. Another tip – Why not institute a silver Challenge Cup for horses regularly hunted and ridden by amateurs to be run for over the old course? Give a replica of the cup and small stake to the winner and advertise well in "The Field" and such like papers. Make every young amateur keen to leave his name on your Cup, and have the same thing for soldier riders on the second day."

Despite Major Longworth's ideas not being implemented, one can appreciate the process of thought which came to fruition in the post-war period following World War II with the introduction of travelling allowances for horses. Whether or not it was as the result of Major Longworth's letter, the stake money for the 1920 meeting was dramatically increased to a total sum of £840. As in the previous year the list of entries for the two days now appeared in the *Totnes Times* several days in advance of the fixture although it could not indicate the number of runners which would actually turn up on the day. It was often the case that an original entry of eight or ten produced a match or a walkover.

The executive were well rewarded for their increase in prizemoney for the 1920 meeting with all races showing marked support by owners with no less than twenty-three entries being received for the Optional Selling Hurdle. The second year of racing after the War had rekindled a resurgence of interest, not only from the racing public but from owners and trainers alike. Sadly, and to prove a point, the number of runners on the two days of the meeting did not reflect the original entry as fields were small, this being attributed to a lengthy spell of fine weather and with the fixture following race meetings at Exeter, Plymouth and Newton Abbot at which many of the same horses were engaged. The first day's racing was memorable in that four out of the five runners in the Somerset Steeplechase took the wrong fence, allowing Tom Fagus to secure a quarter of a mile advantage. Having realised their error the other four set off in hot pursuit. Stick-To-It fell foul of the next fence whilst two continued for a while before giving up, but Lt. Col. A C Little's war charger, Any Time, kept on well and with a late challenge got up to beat Tom Fagus by a head. While he was away on active service, Lt. Col. Little took Any Time to France with him, with the "Regimental Kit", remaining as his charger throughout. When hostilities ceased, racing resumed in Belgium and France, and Any Time, ridden by his owner won many a race 'over the sticks' and on the flat. Since being demobbed the horse had run several times and won half-a-dozen races in the West Country that autumn. Two riders, Mr Jack Anthony and D Dick rode doubles, Anthony on Lady Nelson's Tangerine in the Maiden Hurdle and Mr W A Bankier's Fiddle Bridge in the Handicap Steeplechase, Dick scoring on Mr P Ivall's Manda and Mr H Collins' Canny Bird.

On the second day Lt. Col. Little made a repeat appearance with Any Time in the Open Hunters' Steeplechase for which he walked over. After weighing in he was summoned to the Stewards Room... where he was presented with the silver Cup awarded to the winning rider to the value of twenty guineas, by Mr George Mitchell. Lt. Col. Little responded by saying that he felt very pleased to be receiving such a beautiful cup but rather ashamed to take it without being involved in a race and almost felt like giving it back (but thought better of it – Ed.). His two-day successes, however, did net him £50 for his initial win and the whole stake of £70 for the walkover.

Another jockey of note to ride a winner was L B Rees (a member of the famous racing family) who won the Juvenile Hurdle on Eden Nook. Two years later he was to ride Music Hall to victory in the Grand National of 1922.

It was hardly surprising that the winner of the Selling Steeplechase in 1921 failed to raise a bid at auction as Raeburn's Glass was one of the three contestants who repeatedly refused the open ditch before getting over. He was the mount of Bob Trudgill, a West Country man, who undoubtedly fully earned his riding fee as he did again in 1924 when partnering the 25 to 1 shot, Master Robert, to be first past the post in the Grand National. Upon dismounting he was in a state of collapse due to the stitches which he carried in a leg wound, which had burst open having ridden against doctor's orders. By 1924 standards, he was well rewarded by the horse's owner, Lord Airlie, for his efforts, receiving a cheque for £2,000, a tidy sum in those days. As a postscript, Master Robert who had negotiated thirty of the most fearsome and daunting fences in the world, had run at Totnes two years prior to his Aintree success in the South Devon Handicap Steeplechase, in which he had failed to finish. In all fairness to the horse it was recorded that the gelding had been the victim of interference at a fence which had resulted in the jettisoning of his jockey. In his early years Master Robert was considered far too slow for racing purposes and was used for pulling a plough in County Donegal. His triumph in the Grand National was his swan song being promptly retired by his owner.

The top class jockey, Frank Wootton, paid his first visit to Broadmarsh in

1922 and was rewarded with a winner in the opening race when Glance took the honours in the Optimal Selling Hurdle and was bought in for seventy-five guineas. The jockey again caught the judges' eye on the second day on Yewden in the Juvenile Hurdle. Only two faced the starter for the Selling Steeplchase which developed into a comedy of errors. Tim set off in front but came to grief at the open ditch, cantering off riderless with his jockey in hot pursuit, whilst his rival, Royal Raider, persistently refused. Meanwhile Tim had been recaptured and reunited with his rider, Mr O Stanley, by which time Royal Raider had got underway and was coming up the track. Racing down the course by the river Royal Raider refused again, resulting in the favourite, Tim, regaining the advantage. Having now secured a lead, Royal Raider proceeded to follow Tim to the final fence but could not match the leader's finishing burst on the run to the Post, Tim getting the verdict by three lengths. An objection to the winner was lodged on the grounds of taking the wrong course. This was over-ruled by the Stewards who in all probability were grateful that they were able to declare a winner at all, given the circumstances. The horse was bought in for seventy-five guineas. Our friend, Royal Raider, was to try his luck again on the following day in another two horse contest but was to fare no better in the two-mile Selling Steeplchase, this time falling at the riverside fence to which he had taken a dislike on the previous day, but was remounted to finish in second place.

The 1923 races got off to a poor start with the first and second placed horses in the Selling Hurdle being disqualified for passing the wrong side of a flag. First past the post Grecian Waters had come to the race with an impressive sequence of six successive victories to his name. The eventual winner was Gladease (who had finished third) and was owned by Capt. J B Powell. Bay Powell was a name which was to become even better known on racecourses after World War II. Following the second day's racing the Totnes Times reported that what the Somerset Steeplechase lacked in attractiveness it supplied in amusement as it was again to prove fortunate for Capt. Powell, whose Dick Behan was opposed by only two rivals. White Cockade led to the open ditch where he threw his rider over, while Cash Box refused, Dick Behan continuing to win as he chose, the others returning to the paddock after making several attempts to negotiate the obstacle. Grecian Waters, unlucky loser on the first day, returned to the fray following his disqualification with a three length victory in the Hempston Vale Hurdle then having to survive an objection for interference.

The second day of the 1925 races was notable for the visit of the New Zealand Rugby Football Team, the 'All Blacks', who occupied reserved seating in the grandstand. The press stated that a cordial reception was accorded to the visitors with good wishes for their forthcoming tour in the Motherland. A further observation was that the meeting passed off without a single objection being made, which is so unusual that it is deserving of comment.

Owners whose names were to appear with greater regularity in future years were beginning to recognise Totnes as a suitable venue at which to race their horses, including Mr Herbert G Blagrave, Mr Tom R Rimell, Mr Harry Beeby and Lord Queenborough, whilst Mr Ben Warner was perhaps better known as an owner on the flat.

A further press report of the races tended to state the obvious, recording that when a heavy storm swept over the course before the running of the fifth race it caused an immediate rush for the grandstand, booths, motor cars and any place of shelter. Many of the bookmakers deserted their pitches temporarily and their clients were pleased to keep them company under the big umbrellas until the downpour ceased. Mr G S L Whitelaw's Pullman was the winner of the Selling Hurdle, changing hands at the auction for eighty guineas, his new owner being Mrs M Roberts. In anticipation of a quick return, Mrs Roberts declared the horse to run again the next day in another Selling Hurdle. Shouldering 12st. 7lb. and ridden by Jack Hamey the gelding collected the £50 stake for his owner before again finding a new owner in Mr Merrell.

Bobby Gordon completed a riding double on the second day, Keith Piggott also being on the score sheet. Keith, like his father Ernest before him, rode with a short length of stirrup leather in comparison to his contemporaries. However, both of their styles would have paled into insignificance when compared to that which Andrew Turnell adopted over obstacles some thirty to forty years later not even to the extent of dropping his leathers a hole or two, as many did, when riding at Aintree. To prove this point, Andy Turnell finished third aboard Charles Dickens in the 1974 Grand National. Keith Piggott's son, Lester, was to continue in the same vein on the flat with his own inimitable style which was not to be copied – the closest example being Richard Hughes of the present day jockeys.

An increase in stakes for 1927 saw prizemoney for the two days total over £900. On the track a participant was Mrs Brock's Chambord. Although the five year old was unplaced on the day he was in subsequent years to win his fair share of races at the Devon tracks becoming something of a standing dish at Torquay, where he won four two-mile steeplechases and was second twice. Local interest was served after his racing days were over as being an entire he was retired to stud in the area.

The weather was again a defining influence in the years leading up to the 1930s with long dry spells decimating the size of the fields due to the firm underfoot conditions. The original entry of 180 horses for the twelve races in 1928 was deemed to be highly satisfactory. However, runners on the ground were poor, especially so in 1929 in which five of the twelve contests resulted in walkovers – two on the first day and three on the second. It was, therefore, only to be expected that as a consequence attendances would suffer, especially on the day when only three races were contested.

Totnes was not alone in this situation, as Plymouth Races was reported as being in financial trouble, having lost money over the last three years. Their racecourse lease was due to expire on 25th March 1930 and five of the Committee members who were guarantors stood to lose £1,200. Presumably matters were resolved in the short term, as this fixture went ahead, but it received little support from owners, trainers and the general public. The Committee were to try once again in 1931 but ironically it was flooding on the course that brought about the cancellation of this meeting and which proved to be the final straw. Plymouth Races were never revived. An interesting footnote is that before the first race of the final fixture a sale of horses owned by Mr R Mitchell of Yelverton took place coming under the hammer of auctioneer, Mr John Wakeham.

This was certainly the era of the Piggott brothers, both riding at the peak of their form at Totnes and neighbouring tracks but other names were beginning to appear, as fledglings at the time but who would in the future make huge impacts on the racing scene. One of these was Mr P V F Cazalet, who brought with him a nice young steeplechaser called Youtell, probably a class above the usual type of animal to be found in the area. Ridden by his owner, Youtell won a three mile steeplechase at Exeter by eight lengths, following up with a twenty length victory at Plymouth, before scoring at Totnes in the South Devon Steeplechase by three lengths.

Circumstances had improved by 1931 with more runners than usual which was attributed to the fact that neither Plymouth nor Shirley Races had taken place, forty horses going to post on the first day and forty-eight on the second. It proved to be an excellent two days sport with Mr Faber's Edomite displaying his talents on both, with victories in the Dart Vale Steeplechase over two miles and the South Devon Steeplechase, a three mile event with jockey G. Hardy getting the leg up on each occasion. Other professionals of note to register successes were G Wilson and W Speck.

1932 produced yet another name which in later years was to join the elite list of jump racing's all time 'greats' when amateur rider Mr F T Walwyn was twice seen in the winner's enclosure. On the opening day, he claimed the Bridgetown Handicap Selling Steeplechase on Mr D Thomas' Mayerling after a rare tussle with the runner up to win by three-quarters of a length, then doubling up on Col. M Lindsay's Bluesand, in the Dart Vale Steeplechase, by a more comfortable eight lengths. Fulke Walwyn was to ride Reynoldstown to victory in the Grand National of 1937 – the horse scoring back to back successes, having been partnered by another amateur, Mr Frank Furlong, a brother officer to Walwyn in the 9th Hussars, the previous year. Fulke Walwyn like Peter Cazalet became a superb trainer in later life being destined to turn out scores of big race winners, including many for the Royal family. Team Spirit, by winning the Grand National of 1964, gave Walwyn the rare accolade (later emulated by Fred Winter) of having both ridden and trained a winner of the big race.

The dry weather with its accompanying firm ground returned for the summer of 1933, making life extremely difficult for trainers to prepare their horses. The inevitable consequence was another fixture with small fields. The Somerset Steeplechase was particularly disappointing, attracting only four runners for the three mile contest. The press commented that, "It seems as if this type of staying steeplechase has declined in popularity but that the executive are obliged to stage one such race according to National Hunt regulations".

This time it was the turn of Keith Piggott to collect a riding double, initiated by Tetric in the Selling Hurdle, the second leg coming by way of Peter Murray in the Bridgetown Handicap Steeplechase. Mr Fulke Walwyn continued in winning vein, aboard Scramble in the Novices Hurdle in what was described as a desperate finish. Each day recorded a walkover and it was further noted that not a single fall occurred on either day for which, taking into consideration the state of the going, all riders must have been extremely thankful. The time set for the running of the first race was 3 p.m. which was very unusual for Totnes and it is unclear why this should have been so.

The long drought which prevailed through the summer of 1934 was a source of anxiety to one and all, so the welcome rain which fell ten days prior to the Totnes Races had given hope to those who were afraid that the ground would be too hard for racing. A sum of £860 was on offer for competition and an average size crowd was in attendance with only the second day producing a walkover. This day was marred by the falls in the Town Plate Hurdle of three horses, one of which broke its neck, and which caused the hospitalisation of two jockeys. Bluewhit (K Piggott) and Mileaway were joined by Pied Piper and Harum all being in contention at the last flight where Pied Piper suffered a fatal fall, bringing down Bluewhit and Mileaway. The race was won by Sonna, the mount of F Gurney, by three lengths from Gazonic, with Harum third. Keith Piggott was uninjured but W Redmond (Pied Piper) and B Carter (Mileaway) were transported to the Cottage Hospital.

Apparently the days of the 'Welshing' bookmaker had not yet passed into history, as a *Totnes Times* report detailed the case of Jack Sadler of Manor Park, London, who was brought to trial for his escapades. He was charged with larceny by means of a trick. Mr Sadler had been seen taking bets and was kept under observation by police, when he was seen to cross the leat, take off his coat and mix with the crowd. He was overheard to say, "I'm off", but a policeman brought him back and it was found he could not pay his debts. Sadler admitted to fourteen offences, faced three charges (with eleven others

1982. Mr E J Holman presenting a silver salver to Mrs M Gordon Watson, owner of Sub Rosa, winner of the Totnes Open Hunter Steeplechase, Newton Abbot

1987. Mr R J Michelmore presenting a cut glass decanter to Mr W Bush, owner of Marshlander, winner of the Totnes Open Hunter Steeplechase, Newton Abbot

1988. Maj. R C Niles, C.B.E., presenting a silver salver to Mr G C Fox, owner of Fool's Pleasure, winner of the Totnes Open Hunter Steeplechase, Newton Abbot

Mr J Papworth receiving a silver salver from Mr R Savery following his horse Flying Maria's success in the Totnes Novice Hunter Steeplechase, Newton Abbot, 2001

1997. Mr P J A Wakeham presenting a silver salver to Mr P C Pocock owner of Green Hill, winner of the Totnes Novice Hunter Steeplechase, Newton Abbot, with daughter, Mrs Lynn Jones, trainer (2nd left)
Photo courtesy of Honiton Photographs

1998. Mr R Savery presenting a trophy to Mr C De P Berry, owner of Ardbei, winner of the Restricted race, Dartmoor Point-to-Point, Flete Park

2002. Mr G K M Welch presenting Miss L Gardner with a trophy for the leading Novice lady rider at Flete Park
Photo courtesy of Mark Johnston

Mr R Savery presenting a trophy to Mrs S J Batchelor, owner of Damien's Pride, winner of the Restricted race at Dartmoor Point-to-Point, Flete Park, rider Mr T Dennis, 2002

2005. Mr E J Holman congratulates Miss S Robinson following her success in the Totnes Novice Hunter Steeplechase, Newton Abbot, on John's Legacy

Photo courtesy of Fiona Crawford

Mr R Savery presenting a trophy to Miss M McCarthy, the leading Novice lady rider at Flete Park 2004
Photo courtesy of Mark Johnston

2003. Mr M D Rusden presenting a racewhip to Mr Christian Williams following his success on Jabiru in the Totnes Novice Hunter Steeplechase, Newton Abbot

Mr M D Rusden presenting a trophy to Mr Ross Darke, owner of Eternal Midnight, winner of the Restricted race, Dartmoor Point-to-Point, Flete Park 2009, with rider Mr D Edwards. Photo courtesy of Baths Photographic

CHAPTER 10
PERSONAGES AND PERSONALITIES
IN LATER YEARS

The name of Lt. Col. Harry M Llewellyn will be best remembered in the years which followed the Second World War but as Mr H M Llewellyn he was an accomplished amateur race rider during the 1930s and a visitor to Totnes Races. His mounts were chiefly owned by himself, his father Sir David Llewellyn, or his wife. The degree of his success and ability can be readily assessed by the results achieved. He had ridden the winner of the United Hunts Cup at Cheltenham on his brother's Tapinette and repeated the victory aboard his wife's Bay Marble in 1948. Two days later he won the four mile Foxhunter's Cup on State Control. Twelve years previously he had finished second in the Grand National partnering his father's Ego behind Reynoldstown (Mr F. Walwyn) and again took the ride in 1937 finishing fourth to Royal Mail (Evan Williams). The horse was relatively unfancied at 50 to 1 when beaten twelve lengths by Reynoldstown but was traded as the 10 to 1 second favourite for the return visit. After the war Harry Llewellyn became a household name in equestrian circles and synonymous with British Show Jumping. His magnificent horse, Foxhunter, won the King George V Gold Cup at the White City in 1948. The combination soon became established as members of the British Show Jumping team who were victorious in the Prince of Wales Cup at the Royal International Show and in 1949 travelled to Paris, Nice and Rome together with his other mount, Monty. Foxhunter and his owner were part of the British team which competed in the Seven Nations Cup, visiting Nice, Rome, Madrid, London, Dublin, Ostend and Rotterdam at which venues the team were to acquire three wins, three second places and one third. During this tour Foxhunter did not hit a single fence in any of the Nations Cup competitions. Nevertheless the pair's greatest achievement was yet to come when gaining a gold medal at the Olympic Games in Helsinki in 1952.

Capt. R C (Bobby) Petre was another well known amateur rider on the West Country circuit and at the last fixture to be held at Totnes in 1938 he won the National Hunt Handicap 'Chase on Mr W V Stokes' Tuckmill over three miles, one furlong, and landed a double with the horse on the second day in taking the South Devon Steeplechase over a similar distance. The claret and silver colours of Mr Stokes were to appear again when racing resumed after the war and were carried with distinction for several years thereafter. Bobby Petre ended the season with twenty-one winners and shared the amateur riders' title with Mr A B Mildmay. The first Grand National to be run after the war in 1946 found him aboard Mr J Morant's Lovely Cottage, scoring by four lengths from Jack Finlay with the great Irish steeplechaser, Prince Regent, a further three lengths away in third whilst attempting to concede

25lb. in weight. Bobby Petre turned professional and the following year revisited the scene of his triumph, this time partnering one of Lord Bicester's top class 'chasers, Silver Fame, who was later to win a Cheltenham Gold Cup. Lovely Cottage was an absentee from the race through injury but there was to be no fairytale ending as Silver Fame was among the fallers. Sadly Bobby Petre's career as a jockey was short lived, for having survived the war years - he served with the Scots Guards – and the perils of the racecourse, he slipped on a breakwater fracturing a leg so badly that it had to be amputated.

My third personage to feature in this chapter was almost certainly to become the best known and best loved amateur jockey in the history of National Hunt racing. Mr Anthony Bingham Mildmay, as he then was, was the product of a family steeped in the history of steeplechasing. His father, Mr Francis B Mildmay, M.P., had been a keen supporter and Steward of Totnes and Bridgetown Races in earlier days and his relationship to the Bulteel family can only have enhanced his sporting interest and desire to become a jockey. Standing six feet two inches in height and having to hone his frame down to a weight of ten stone cannot have been easy but nevertheless that is what he achieved when embarking upon a racing career, riding his first winner under rules in 1933 when Good Shot won at Wye. The same year, at twenty-four years of age, he had his first ride in the Grand National aboard Youtell who fell at the first fence. Two years later he returned to Aintree this time riding Master Orange who fared little better also being a faller. A third attempt in 1936 when partnering his father's Davy Jones will be remembered as a supreme example of the misfortune that at times is synonymous with horse racing, for having jumped the penultimate fence with the race apparently at his mercy the reins parted at the buckle end, leaving the rider with no control over his mount who ran out at the final fence. The resulting media coverage did, however, bring to the attention of the public the skills and ability of this promising young amateur rider. History was to repeat itself in an even more bizarre fashion in the Grand National of 1956, twenty years later, when Devon Loch and Dick Francis had victory snatched away within sight of the winning post, the loser receiving far more attention than the victor. Unlike Anthony Mildmay, Dick Francis was already well established as a Champion Jockey and the ultimate professional.

Anthony Mildmay was a great supporter of his local West Country tracks at which he was the recipient of a loyal and enthusiastic following by race goers. His appearances at Totnes were greeted with anticipation of further successes and on the last day on which the races were to be run, 1st September 1938, he signed off with a winner, the French-bred grey mare, Nouvelle Mode, in the South Hams Optional Selling Steeplchase. During the war years he served in the Commandos, Welsh Guards and the Guards Armoured Division. His racing colours of light blue and white were becoming increasingly familiar on British racecourses and when racing resumed in 1946 his career in the saddle blossomed. Having shared the amateur riders' title with Bobby Petre before the war he became the outright Champion in the 1946-47 season with thirty-two winners and remained the leading amateur rider up to his death. His greatest wish was to win the Grand National and having inherited his peerage in 1947 he returned to Liverpool in 1948 for the big race in which he had two runners, Ultra Bene who was ridden by Tony Grantham and Cromwell, the better fancied of the pair, which he was to ride himself. History records that the combination finished third in the race to Sheila's Cottage, but that Cromwell's chances were not helped in the latter stages of the race, Lord Mildmay having suffered an attack of cramp to his neck, the site of an old injury, which prevented him rendering his horse any assistance in the critical final mile. Ultra Bene, the second string was one of the fallers. Cromwell and his owner were to return to the scene again in 1949 and 1950, finishing fourth and falling at the third attempt.

Lord Mildmay's tragic death on 12th May 1950 was a serious loss to the racing scene. He was a member of the National Hunt Committee and a local Steward. During his career in the saddle he was in demand from many well known owners and trainers of the day. He had scored on Jack Tatters for Hon. Dorothy Paget and had been successful on Castledermot in the four mile National Hunt Steeplchase at the Cheltenham Festival for the legendary Dr Vincent O'Brien. His influence and friendship with the Royal family resulted in the visit of H.R.H. Princess Margaret to Buckfastleigh races in 1948.

One of the best known of professional jockeys who rode at Totnes between the two Wars was Gerald Wilson. He will always be remembered through his association with the mighty Golden Miller, being one of the five different pilots engaged by Miss Dorothy Paget to partner the horse in the Cheltenham Gold Cup between 1932 and 1938. At least Gerry Wilson retained the ride to score in the consecutive years of 1934 and 1935 whilst the other jockeys were only granted a single opportunity. Wilson went on to win the Grand National on 'The Miller', as he was known, to complete the Gold Cup double in 1934, the only horse to have achieved this feat. He had come to prominence in 1931 when booked to ride Coup de Chapeau in the Champion Steeplchase at Liverpool in which the horse dead heated for first place with Easter Hero. This was the beginning of a long and distinguished career which saw him become Champion Jockey on seven occasions between 1933 and 1941. He was very much in form when visiting Totnes on the first day of the 1938 meeting riding a double in the two hurdle races with Abbot's Glance and Proud Moment. Many retired jockeys embark upon a training career but Gerry Wilson's was short lived, taking out a licence in the curtailed 1944-45 season. By 1956 he was 'mine host' of a public house and died in 1968 at the relatively young age of sixty-five.

Keith Piggott was the son of Ernest, whom we have already encountered in an earlier chapter as a frequent visitor to Totnes races in his role as a jump jockey before the First World War. Keith was the better known of the two brothers, Victor being somewhat less successful as a rider. Keith Piggott was to ride his first steeplechase winner in 1923 at Quorn Hunt (Loughborough), which unlike its title was a licensed racecourse and not a track used for point to point racing. Born in 1904 the young Piggott was to become a familiar figure at West Country meetings. He had gained notable success when partnering Vaulx to victory in the Welsh Grand National of 1925 when still only twenty years of age. The race in those days used to be run at Cardiff and in recent times has been housed at Chepstow, the Cardiff racecourse closing one year after Totnes in 1939. He was not to be blessed with the same level of success at Liverpool as that enjoyed by his father who had won three Nationals. Keith was to have five attempts at the premier prize as a jockey but failed to finish on each occasion. He was to have marginally better luck in the Cheltenham Gold Cup, finishing in third place on Grakle behind Easter Hero in 1929, and the next year improved his placing when runner up on the same horse in 1930, with Easter Hero again being too good. Keith Piggott fared even better at Plymouth races than Totnes especially at their farewell meeting in 1930 when he recorded three wins, two seconds and two thirds from his seven mounts. His riding career, which ended with the outbreak of World War II, saw him notch over 500 winners in total. The Aintree bogey which had denied him a success in the big race as a jockey was remedied to a certain degree when, as trainer and co-owner of Ayala in 1963, the gelding triumphed in the hands of Pat Buckley to add Keith Piggott's name to the Grand National roll of honour. Keith was the father of Lester, the most famous of all the flat race jockeys, both in this country and on the international stage in the twentieth century.

There have been many colourful characters who have graced the turf but in all probability none more so in the literal sense than the tipster who operated not only in this country but also on the continent and who styled himself as Ras Prince Monolulu. Between the wars he travelled by rail to ply his trade at the Devon meetings including Totnes and Newton Abbot. Monolulu was a tall, dark, woolly-haired man, clad in flowing robes with a headdress of multicoloured feathers. He was to be seen not only on the racecourse but in the streets and markets of London for nearly fifty years. His famous raucous cry of "I've gotta horse" was heard wherever he appeared. At one time in the 1930s he had amassed a fortune of £150,000 from his wagers but six months later was virtually penniless. His dress of gaily coloured pantaloons with a decorative waistcoat and plumed headdress earned him his place among the records of the most famous men on the turf. He claimed to be of Abyssinian origin although his papers were registered in the name of Peter Mackay. In all probability it was as much an assumed name as Ras Prince Monolulu, Chief of the Abyssinian tribe of Falasha. Whilst working the London markets he would often end up in the police courts on various charges. It is true that he knew many leading owners and jockeys of the day and was courted by the media. Most Epsom Derbys featured his photograph in the next day's newspapers and he appeared on the 'newsround' of television which was then in its infancy. His patter included the phrases, "White man for pluck, black man for luck", and "God made the bees, the bees make the honey, the public back the favourite, the bookies take the money". Another version of this ditty ran, "Birds will sing and bells will ring, and the bees will make the honey, punters always study form, but the bookies take the money". His overnight accommodation depended upon his success or lack of it on the racecourse. He recalls that when visiting Totnes or Newton Abbot all lodgings were full to capacity and that he ended up sleeping in the workhouse as there was nowhere else to go. He claimed to be on speaking terms with the Prince of Wales (Duke of Windsor) and the Aga Khan. Monolulu was in demand by radio producers and appeared in such shows as *Shipmates Ashore* with Doris Hare and *Navy Mixture* with Bonar Colleano and Benny Lee. He made money and stayed at the best hotels, he lost money and slept where he could, but what is undeniable is that racecourse characters such as Ras Prince Monolulu who had appeared on tracks from the 1920s through to the 1950s have passed into history. I do not recall seeing or hearing of him on West Country racecourses after the Second World War but I did see him in all his glory at Windsor Races in 1952.

I conclude this chapter by selecting a quartet of personages: two professional jockeys, one owner and amateur rider, and a racing family, each of whom had connections to Totnes Races. The Epsom-based jockey, Frank Wootton, who paid his first visit to the course in 1922, had an illustrious riding career on the flat, firstly holding the highest number of winners for an apprentice until the advent of Lester Piggott. He was at the time hailed as the greatest jockey to have left Australia; he had been Champion there in successive years, 1909-12. Undoubtedly this claim could well have been challenged in later years having regard to the exploits of Arthur (Scobie) Breasley and William Raphael (Rae) Johnstone. Frank Wootton won the Oaks on Perola (1909) and the St. Leger on Swynford (1910). He was noted for his liking of sticking to the inside rail in races. In his early years he weighed just a trifle over 6 st. when winning the Cesarewitch on Denmure (1907) and again three years later on Verney. He was also successful in prominent races such as the Chester Cup, the Ascot Stakes and the Manchester Cup. When no longer able to ride at the required weights for flat racing he turned his attention to hurdle racing. Like a handful of other post war riders such as Dennis Dillon, Johnny Gilbert and Harry Sprague (with a very occasional exception) he confined himself to competing over the minor obstacles.

Fred Rimell was the Champion National Hunt Jockey on four occasions, twice before the war, following in the footsteps of his brother-in-law, Gerry Wilson, the first Championship coming in 1938-39 with seventy-one winners. He gained his initial success on the flat at Chepstow as an apprentice at the age of twelve, and went on to score thirty-four victories on the level. He acquired his second crown in the season 1939-40 and when racing resumed in 1944-45 he shared the honours with H (Frenchie) Nicholson before winning outright in 1945-46. He had learnt his trade with his father, Tom, at Kinnersley which was to continue as his base when he became a trainer. The stable had turned out Forbra to win the 1932 Grand National, trained by Tom Rimell. Fred was to break his neck in a fall at Wincanton in 1946 from which he recovered, but the following season he suffered an even more severe fall in the Cheltenham Gold Cup from Coloured School Boy which resulted in a broken back. This was to be his last race ride. His career as a trainer was to achieve even greater heights, by collecting two Cheltenham Gold Cups, three Champion hurdles and four Grand Nationals besides heading the Trainers' Championship.

The 1926 Totnes race card included two entries, Newtown Wonder and Irish Prince, in the ownership of Major D G Campbell. Neither were to win their respective races, Newtown Wonder achieved the better result by finishing third in the two mile Handicap Steeplechase, both being ridden by a professional jockey. It was in the years prior to 1896 that David Campbell had begun to make a name for himself as an amateur rider under Rules, chiefly through his purchase of an unbroken bay gelding, bred by Pat Doyle in Ireland, for a modest sum. Introduced to the racecourse and named The Soarer, he won no fewer than seven times over fences as a five year old, partnered by his owner who was a member of the 9th Lancers. During the next season the horse became difficult to train, in consequence of which he was passed on to Mr Hall Walker for the sum of £500 with the proviso that David Campbell could have the ride in the 1896 Grand National. The Soarer's form prior to the big race did not inspire much confidence, with only one victory in eleven starts. The race itself was to belie the form book with the horse winning by a margin of 1½ lengths from Father O'Flynn. The fortunate owner, who was later to become Lord Wavertree, had invested a £50 wager on his 40 to 1 chance. The Soarer and Campbell were to attempt a repeat performance the following year but to no avail, the partnership falling at Valentine's Brook and giving David Campbell, who had obtained special leave from India to take the ride, a broken collar bone. He was nevertheless the first serving cavalry officer to win the big race and was in command of the 9th Lancers, which regiment he took to France in 1914, later retiring from the army when in command at Aldershot. Following promotion and acquiring an honour, General Sir David Campbell died in 1936. Local interest was served in that his son, Major

General Victor D G Campbell was for many years domiciled at South Brent and was the step-father of Jennifer, Mrs Robert Savery, whose husband is a Director of Totnes and Bridgetown Races Company.

Point-to-points are frequently credited as being the nursery for National Hunt racing with many an owner, rider, official and horse cutting their teeth in the amateur ranks before joining the professional scene. So it was in the case of Mr and Mrs A J Renfree and family, whose horses first appeared on the West Country circuit in 1937 gaining early success. Based at St. Mellion, Cornwall, Alfred Renfree and his wife built up a useful string of horses, many of them acquired from selling races, and which he frequently improved with his training methods to justify their purchase. Although many were to compete in the lower grade races, the winners began to accumulate. They were initially trained under permit with a professional licence being taken out some twenty years later. Early runners from the stable included Pat O'Shaugnessy, Skrun Bridge, Princess Avril, Long Look, Brandy Boy, Gallent and Breadcrust. During the post war years the family were to play ever increasing roles in the management and running of the yard with the three children, Mollie, James (Jim) and Jennifer, being actively involved. This trio were to commence their racing careers in point-to-points, the eldest Mollie riding several winners between the flags, but it was Jim and Jennifer who were to enjoy the best results. Both were natural light weights, Jim having no difficulty in riding at the minimum of 10st. (and below in his claiming days). Clapper Bridge was to give him his first point-to-point win and Golden Kippers, the first under Rules. He was to become one of the leading amateur riders in the country before joining the professional ranks. A steady stream of runners emanated from the stable and the yellow and black colours of his father were among the best known in the locality. All the horses were cheaply bought, many of them at the Ascot sales, with such well known performers as Sea Fury, War Whoop, John O'Groats (who was to win the Whitbread Gold Cup in different ownership), Dos de Junio, Pantalon II, Step On It, Sanscrit and Vertu, being regular visitors to the winners enclosure. Belljinks proved to be a shrewd addition to the string winning several three mile steeplechases often under big weights. Le Voyageur who had been a seasoned campaigner in his prime joined the Renfree establishment as a veteran and was rejuvenated to be one of the best point-to-pointers in the area.

Jennifer's talents were confined to this code, as ladies were not yet permitted to ride under Rules. Her abilities were soon recognised by owners who were only too eager to snap up her services when she was available and not required to ride her father's entries. Mr Reg Shilston's Sunnyminosa was one of her successful outside rides but she will forever be associated with Mr W J Rogers' amazing pony, Lonesome Boy, who won pony races over fences and was invincible in Ladies Races over banks, scoring on sixty-five occasions of which his last fifty-three were successive, two records which I confidently predict will be everlasting. Jennifer Renfree was in the saddle for the majority of his wins, with Mrs Diana Coaker replacing her during the final season and Mr Frank Ryall getting the leg up over fences. She was the National Point to Point Champion Lady Rider on five occasions, 1954, 1955, 1956, sharing the title in 1957 and 1958. Jennifer was to marry Mr David Barons and together they set up a training establishment near Kingsbridge to which she brought her expertise to create one of the more notable success stories in National Hunt racing from just a nucleus of two horses, Legend Prince and Le Voyageur, during the first year of their marriage.

The colourful and most famous tipster of them all – Ras Prince Monolulu

CHAPTER 11
THE COMPANY, SPONSORSHIP AND DINNERS
(1940 - 2009)

In 1940 consideration was still being given to the possibility of holding a race meeting, probably because racing was continuing at Torquay and Newton Abbot. However, the suggestion was rejected as being impracticable in the prevailing circumstances. The grazing on the marshes was let to Mr J H Connabeer, together with part of the Weir Marsh, owned by the West of England Bacon factory and rented by the Race Company. The Surveyor, Mr A S Brook, reported that the Town Council had deposited a quantity of animal bones in the saddling stalls. It was agreed that Mr Brook contact the Borough Engineer to inform him that in future bones must not be brought to the paddock as it could encourage the presence of rats and other vermin; also to point out that owing to some of the horse boxes being so tightly packed with paper (being collected for the war effort), the doors were being strained and that he give the matter his urgent attention.

The weighing room was being used by the Home Guard as a Guard Room. The grazier complained that the main entrance gate was being left open by walkers and that his cattle were in danger of straying on to the railway line. It was decided that a padlock and chain be fixed to the gate to prevent trespassing. An application from the military authorities for the use of sixteen loose boxes was granted together with the fodder store and harness room as part of a requisitioning order from the War Department. A further order was received the following year from the Chief Billeting Officer taking possession of all the unoccupied accommodation on the racecourse. This resulted in alterations being carried out to the premises for the accommodation of workmen employed in the shipbuilding yard of Messrs F Curtis & Co. Totnes Town Council requested rental of the Company's land at Weir Marsh for the purpose of creating a bathing facility. This was agreed at a fee of £5 per annum. It was also intimated that the Admiralty would be taking over the premises from the local Chief Billeting Officer; a bomb crater was in evidence on this Marsh due to enemy action on 21st October 1942.

1943 brought to an end the long reign of John Mason as both the Committee and the Company's Secretary. His death being recorded after thirty-five years of service prompted the appointment of Mr A S (Togo) Brook as Acting Secretary until racing was resumed, which as events transpired was an open ended commitment. The Company decided to sell its Austin van and thirty-five iron hurdles and the following year wrote to the National Hunt Committee seeking advice on the future of the present racecourse and the possible requisition of another within the Totnes area. A letter was also written to Messrs Michelmore, Loveys & Sons, Agents to the Duke of Somerset, and to Major Sir Samuel Harvey asking for permission to view parcels of land on their Berry Pomeroy and Harberton estates to see if it were possible to select an area which could be used as a racecourse, should the Admiralty decide that the existing marshes were impossible to reinstate for further racing activities at the end of their occupation. Capt. F J C Holdsworth together with Messrs A Hingston, J G Kellock and W R Holman were elected to view the country in the Dundridge and Luscombe Cross areas as being possible sites for a proposed racecourse.

1948 brought a letter from the Admiralty offering to purchase the racecourse. Due to the activities carried out in connection with the war effort, in particular with regard to the amount of bulldozing undertaken in respect of the building of barges and other naval craft, the course was left in a general state of dereliction. A Bailey bridge had been constructed and slung across the River Dart to afford access from the Totnes-Newton Abbot road, this still being in place. The Company replied stating that they would be prepared to sell all the land on the east side of the Mill Leat including the Weir field, north of the railway line to which access was under the Great Western Railway and across the racecourse, this being the only approach for cattle. The Company would like to retain the paddock from the turnstile entrance to the north end of the weighing room and all the premises, providing compensation was paid for their reinstatement but would wish to include the grandstand and land adjoining in the sale of the land on the east side of the Leat. It was proposed that the Secretary write to the land agents of Sir Samuel Harvey to enquire if there was a possibility of purchasing or renting a site for a proposed racecourse on Gerston Farm, the site having been viewed by the Directors. Arrangements were put in hand to hold a Company Dinner (the first of several) at the Seven Stars Hotel in December with the guest list to include the Duke of Somerset, Lord Mildmay of Flete, Mr H F Brunskill, Major F Passey, Sir Samuel Harvey, Dr S C Jellicoe, Mr E T Cox, Mr H Fielding, Mr J Wakeham and Mr D Mann.

The negotiations with the Admiralty still rumbled on without conclusion. The Directors were of the opinion that the exhorbitant cost of reinstatement to the Company precluded any likely return of the land being used for racing purposes. Sites in the Totnes area had been viewed but appeared to be unsuitable for a racecourse. It is somewhat ironical that eleven years hence, in 1957, the Dart Vale and Haldon Harriers were to hold their point-to-point races on a track at Gerston Farm and later on at another course at Bowden Pillars. Racing was to resume on other courses in Devon, at Newton Abbot, Buckfastleigh and Devon & Exeter, although the war years had witnessed the demise of Torquay in 1940, Plymouth having already succumbed to economic pressures after the abandonment of their 1931 fixture.

The Company loaned equipment to both the Dart Vale Harriers and the

South Devon Foxhounds for use at their point-to-point races, also to the National Hunt meetings at Buckfastleigh and Newton Abbot. Although having no active racecourse of their own the Board of Directors affirmed that their one object, although being limited by guarantee, was to promote and foster horse racing, breeding and other similar sport within the area, a sentiment which remains in operation to the present day. A request from Totnes Town Council for permission to plant trees on the tongue of land on the north side of Totnes Bridge was granted.

Agreement was finally reached with the Admiralty in 1949 for the sale of all the racecourse land and buildings, with the exception of the portion of Weir Field amounting to some two acres rented by the Town Council and used for bathing and as a sports field. Settlement was achieved at the sum of £8,000 but final contracts were not exchanged for another twelve months for the 28¾ acres. The Town Council enquired as to the possibility of acquiring a lease on part of Weir Fields for a number of years as they had been approached by Totnes Association Football Club for an extension to their occupation. The Company refused but indicated that they would be prepared to sell for £300. They also forwarded letters to the Secretaries of Newton Abbot and Buckfastleigh Races with the offer of donating a silver cup to the value of £25 for competition in a Hunters Steeplechase during the 1950 season. This was to herald an association with Buckfastleigh Races which endured up to its closure in 1960 and an even longer and on-going relationship with Newton Abbot whose calendar includes the annual staging of the Totnes and Bridgetown Hunter Steeplechase to which the Company donates a trophy, usually in the form of a silver salver, to the winning owner and in recent years a whip to the successful rider. The original cost of £25 for the 1950 silver cup has increased by at least a multiple of twelve. Support in the form of sponsorship for hunter steeplechasing at Devon & Exeter (now Exeter) has been more intermittent but a Totnes and Bridgetown Hunter Steeplechase is currently run at Exeter Racecourse. It was also agreed to donate a silver cup to the Dart Vale and Haldon Harriers for their Members' Race in 1952.

Totnes Town Council enquired as to whether the Company would extend the lease held by them for the use of part of Weir Marsh field to fourteen years, as the West of England Bacon factory was not prepared to sell their portion of land but would be happy to grant a lease for a similar period.

The Directors decided to hold another Dinner at the Seven Stars Hotel which would incorporate the handing over of the Hunter Steeplechase trophies to the representatives from Buckfastleigh and Newton Abbot. The guest list would include Brigadier J N Lumley, Mr C L Vicary, Mr A C Bulpin Snr., Mr R Hoare, Mr R Loveband, Mr W E Coulton, Mr J Coulton, Mr N G Coulton, Mr C W Best, Mr J R Warren, Lord Mildmay, Col. A C Vicary, Mr J Wakeham, Mr H G Michelmore and Major E C Weldon.

The Board of Directors were to suffer two losses in 1951 with the resignation of Major W G Loveys and the death of Capt. F J C Holdsworth. Major Lovey's vacancy was filled by Mr Bryan L Toll, whilst the following year the Board lost Mr George Burton Marks, who had been a Director since 1938 and had hosted many Company meetings at his home at No. 33 Fore Street. The death in 1952 was also announced of Mr John Wakeham, whose association with the racecourse as Starter and Auctioneer had commenced in 1920.

Equipment still in the possession of the Company was always in demand and the Minutes record that loans were made to the South Devon Hunt point to point, the local Pony Club, Ilsington Parish Sports Society's Sheep Dog Trials and Totnes and Bridgetown Regatta Committee.

The Directors suffered yet another loss in 1953 with the passing of Mr Alfred Hingston who had been a member of the Board since 1929. Mr Sydney Morgan was appointed in his place whilst Mr Sidney Burton Marks was to replace his father. Sadly this latter appointment was to be only short lived as Mr Marks' death occurred just two years later. A donation of £5 was made to the South Devon Hunt towards a fund to purchase a memorial silver cup for competition at their point-to-point in recognition of the services to the races of Mr Charles Lane Vicary. An extra cup was donated to the Buckfastleigh Races as the running of the Hunter 'Chase in 1953 had resulted in a dead heat between Phil's Castle and Cabin Hill. However, it was stipulated that in future, in the event of a dead heat, the owners must decided between themselves who would receive the trophy!

During the previous year the Admiralty had re-sold the old racecourse land and buildings to Staverton Builders who offered to buy the Company's half of Weir Marsh for £150. This offer was declined as insufficient and as the land was under lease to the Town Council.

In 1957 the deaths were reported of three Directors: Lt. Col. Francis K Windeatt, who had been a member of the old Race Committee and had been Chairman of the Company since 1934, Mr William Robert Holman, a Director since 1932 and Mr Sidney Burton Marks. The next year, Dr A McDowell Davies was to fill the vacancy created by Lt. Col. Windeatt, Mr E J Holman replaced his late father, and Mr Roger J Michelmore took the place of Mr Marks. Mr Joseph G Kellock was elected as Chairman, a position he was to occupy for the next twenty-four years.

Rumours were circulating in 1958 concerning the future of Buckfastleigh Races. The Company sent a letter to the Races Secretary, Mr Guy Coulton, with the offer that should the question of his executive being required or desiring to purchase their racecourse and should they require financial assistance the Directors would be prepared to consider the matter of helping. Sadly the course was to close in 1960.

Horse racing has always been a high risk sport to both horse and rider and so it proved in 1959 with the death of professional and well-known jockey, Michael Pumfrey, following a fall at Newton Abbot Races which occurred at the fence alongside the river bank. A memorial fund was opened in favour of his widow to which the Totnes Directors subscribed. It was decided to hold a Dinner in 1960 to which representatives from the executives of Newton Abbot, Devon & Exeter and Buckfastleigh should be invited with Col. Sir John G Carew Pole as Chief Guest and Speaker. The guest list included Mr G W Whitton, Mr W A Anstey and Mr T G Cundy (Devon & Exeter), Mr W E Coulton, Mr John Coulton, Mr Guy Coulton and Mr J R Warren (Buckfastleigh), Cmdr. R J B Mildmay-White, Mr A C Bulpin Snr., Mr A C Bulpin Jnr., and Mr C C Whitley (Newton Abbot). Totnes and Bridgetown Directors who attended were Mr J G Kellock, Mr B L Toll, Mr S N Morgan, Mr E J Holman, Dr A McDowell Davies, Mr R J Michelmore and the Company Secretary, Mr A S Brook.

A change in the Regulations concerning point-to-point racing in 1961 prohibited the customary award of a valuable trophy to the winning owner. All such trophies now had to become perpetual, although an accompanying replica or memento was permissible. The Company then donated a silver cup to the Dart Vale and Haldon Harriers for competition in their Members' Race together with a memento in the form of a travelling clock, their meeting being held at Gerston Farm, Totnes.

By 1962 the sale of Dean Court Farm had taken place and although the Buckfastleigh Races executive had attended, they were unable to effect a purchase, having to concede to the superior bid of a Property Company. At a subsequent auction sale Mr G H Nickels of Maidencombe, Torquay, a South Devon farmer, acquired the racecourse, ancillary land and buildings including the grandstand, amounting to some 133 acres for the sum of £15,250. The property had originally been sold on behalf of Lord Churston and formed part of the Dean Court Estate. Mr Kellock reported to the Company that he had enquired from Mr Nickels as to whether he would be prepared to lease the land to Totnes and Bridgetown Race Company as it was public knowledge that Mr Nickels' application to the Stewards of the National Hunt Committee for a licence to permit the course to be re-opened had been refused. Mr Nickels had intimated that he would be prepared to listen to any proposal. Mr Kellock had been approached by some local hunts to see if arrangements could be made for point-to-point races to be run over the course. He further reported that he had been in contact with a local farmer at Dean Prior who was prepared to rent the grazing for the sum of £750 per annum, with Mr Nickels requiring a rent of £1,000 per year.

The Directors agreed that there was a basis for negotiation and that each participating hunt should be invited to pay a small rental fee for the privilege of racing and a share of the expenses of building and rigging the course, together with 25% of their net profit over the average of their three previous meetings, this sum to form a reserve fund on which to draw in case of emergencies. The Company agreed that the Chairman (Mr Kellock) should proceed with negotiations with the landlord in respect of a lease also with Mr R Coulton for the grazing. A meeting was held at Allerton, the home of Mr Kellock, with representatives of the Dartmoor Foxhounds, Mid Devon Foxhounds, Dart Vale and Haldon Harriers and the South Pool Harriers. Representing the Company were Mr Kellock, Mr Morgan and Mr Brook, whilst Capt. W G Peek, Cmdr. M T Collier (Dartmoor), Mr C P Hooley (Mid Devon), Mr J D Warren, Miss E Frost (Dart Vale and Haldon) and Maj. A W Rainey (South Pool) were also in attendance. After outlining the proposals the Totnes and Bridgetown representatives left the meeting and upon their return, Capt. Peek as spokesman for the four hunts said that all were unanimous in their willingness to participate in the scheme, with the first fixtures to be held in 1963. The Directors would appoint their own Clerk of the Course, Mr E J (Ted) Holman, who would liaise with an Assistant Clerk appointed by each hunt. There would be three point-to-points held during the year with the two Harrier packs sharing a meeting. The present landlords of the Racecourse were Dean Park Investments (Buckfast) Ltd. and through their solicitor Mr A J Boyce (Torquay), indicated that they were prepared to sell certain equipment which they had purchased from Buckfastleigh Race Company, the Directors agreeing to such a purchase.

A subsequent meeting of the Company was held at Buckfastleigh Racecourse which was attended by Mr J D Warren (Dart Vale and Haldon), Mr R N Widdicombe (South Pool), Mr J Thomas (Dartmoor) and Mr Coode (Dean Park Investments) to finalise arrangements. A further offer by the Company to Mr Boyce was made for the purchase of all the remaining race equipment including the weighing scales, turnstiles, hurdles, flags, etc. which was agreed. As the first point-to-point to be held on the course (Dart Vale and Haldon and South Pool) on 23rd March was two days before Mr John Coulton relinquished his tenancy, his permission was sought and obtained. Mr Coulton whose family had been associated with Buckfastleigh Races since 1890 was to move to Bilberryhill in the same parish, once the home of Mr Joseph Hamlyn whose horses were a familiar sight at Totnes Races nearly a century before. By 1963 Broadmarsh had been considerably developed into an industrial estate and was home to the new Totnes Cattle Market.

A very large crowd was in attendance at the first point-to-point to be held at Buckfastleigh, in fact the largest ever seen at the time on the South West point-to-point circuit, although smaller in comparison to the vast numbers who had attended Buckfastleigh Races in 1948 with the visit of Princess Margaret.

Press and television coverage played their part together with the general enthusiasm of the racing public who were only too pleased to welcome the return of horse racing to the course after an interval of three years. The point to point Secretary for the initial fixture was Miss Elizabeth Frost (now Mrs Duggleby) who with her husband, has been such a help to me in compiling this book.

A letter was received from Totnes Town Council seeking to terminate the lease which they held on the land at Weir Marsh which had been used by Totnes Town Football Club in recent years. An enquiry had come to hand from the Unigate milk factory which adjoined the land as to whether the Company were prepared to sell. The resulting sale severed the remaining link of the Company with its racecourse at Broadmarsh.

Changes to the Board of Directors took place in 1965 with the resignation of Mr Sydney Morgan. Mr Bryan Toll was appointed as Vice-Chairman to Mr Kellock and Mr Ted Holman relinquished his position as Clerk of the Course at Buckfastleigh Racecourse after getting the early point-to-point meetings 'up and running'. His replacement was Mr Ralph Widdicombe who was to take up the reins in 1967. This was the year of the expiry of the lease which the Company had negotiated with Mr Harry Nickels and which they were not seeking to renew. However, it transpired that Mr Nickels was not prepared to enter into an agreement with the local hunts on an individual basis, so the Company would therefore explore the possibility of a further renewal for a three year period from 25th March 1967 to 28th January 1970 with the right to hold meetings up to 24th April 1970. Messrs R Coulton & Son were happy to continue as graziers of the land.

The company was to suffer another loss in 1967 with the death of the Vice-Chairman, Mr Bryan Toll, a Director since 1952. His replacement was local businessman, Maj. R C Niles. The following year the Company embraced sponsorship at point-to-point races for the first time in contrast to being just a donor of trophies. The King's Cup (the trophy having been donated by King George VI) was an Adjacent Hunts race run at the Dartmoor and Modbury point-to-point and this sponsorship was to continue in the ensuing years. A silver cigarette box was given for the West of England Hunter Steeplechase at Devon & Exeter with a silver cup presented to the Dart Vale and Haldon Harriers for competition at their hunter trials. 1968 also saw the election of Mr Roger Michelmore as Vice-Chairman to succeed Mr Toll.

In 1970 the tenancy of Buckfastleigh Racecourse from Mr Harry Nickels was renewed for a further three years. Mr Ralph Widdicombe resigned from his office as Clerk of the Course due to ill health, the new appointee being Mr Ivor Lang. Mr Widdicombe was later to become a Jockey Club Inspector of point-to-point courses in the area.

It was decided to hold another Dinner (they were instigated approximately every three years) as an expression of thanks by the Company to persons who had made a contribution to horse racing, hunting or as landowners who were supportive. This year the venue was the Chateau Bellevue at Totnes (formerly Bourton Hall) and, in addition to the Directors, invitations were sent to Mr A C Bulpin, Mr C C Whitley, Mr C Nekola (representing Newton Abbot Races), Brig. Sir Ralph Rayner, Mr T F H Garratt and Lt. Col. A L Trundle (Devon & Exeter), also Mr G H Nickels, Mr R N Widdicombe and Mr I S G Lang.

The Buckfastleigh lease was due for renewal in 1973 and agreement was reached for an extension of a further two years instead of three. The landlord retained possession of the three acre field which lay between the entrance and the lower range of horse stables but granted permission to race over it. It was agreed that a race whip should be presented to the leading rider at the three meetings at Buckfastleigh as indeed had been done the previous year. Due to the increasing cost of silver it was resolved that silver plate trophies should be considered for awards in the future. This resolution was never implemented.

By 1975 the racecourse lease was nearing expiry but the Chairman stated that he had been able to reach an understanding with Mr Nickels for an extension of another two years. Mr R S Coulton had declined to rent the grazing.It was subsequently let to Mr R B Rogers of Buckfastleigh for approximately double the price. Part of the grandstand needed to be fenced off due to defective flooring, some of the timbers showing signs of rot. Mr Nickels had built a new bungalow on the retained field just below the main entrance but it was possible to continue the race track past it, but in close proximity to the front garden.

Following the three meetings Mr Nickels contacted the Company to inform them that he was putting the property on the market, the sale to be conducted by Messrs Rendells (Auctioneers) of Newton Abbot. The sale would comprise either the whole of the land which would include the field spanning the hill up to the slate quarry on the south side of the racecourse, or in part with the course being a separate lot. This would include the new bungalow. The Directors expressed interest with a view to assembling a consortium of people who might be interested in purchasing the property. The Totnes Board were not in a position to purchase themselves, but were anxious to do what they could in order for point-to-point racing to continue. With the intention of bringing interested parties together a private meeting was convened at the Seymour Hotel, Totnes, as Mr Nickels had stated that it was his intention to put the land to auction in the Spring of 1976. At the meeting the following persons were present: for the Company: Mr Kellock (Chairman), Mr R J Michelmore, Dr A McDowell Davies, Mr I S G Lang and Mr A S Brook. Others with interest including the participating hunts were Mr J A Budgett, Mr S Foale, Mrs J G Kellock. Capt. W G Peek, Cmdr. M T Collier, Mr and Mrs Gordon Hall, Mr M B Ogle, Mrs J G Scott, Mr P J A Wakeham,

Mr R N Widdicombe, Mr M D Rusden, Mr A P Moore, Mr A D Hurn, Mr D Allen, Mr P Franklin, Mrs J Pinsent, Mr J Lapthorne, Mr J A Darke, Mr R H Luscombe, Mr J H Cockrem, Mr A Goddard, Mr M C Chaplin, Mr M Mortimore, Mr F Hutchings and Mr J MacClean. It was agreed that a further meeting be called when more details were to hand in a month's time. Present at the reconvening were Messrs Kellock, Holman, Michelmore, Dr Davies, Messrs Niles, Brook, Lang, Mildmay-White, Cockrem, Cmdr. Collier, Mrs Kellock, Messrs Rusden, Wakeham, Scott, Widdicombe, Goddard, Darke, Luscombe, Chaplin, Maj. Rainey and Mr and Mrs Hurn.

As there was insufficient financial support forthcoming it was decided to form a sub-committee to discuss the particulars of sale when published. The sub-committee consisted of, for the Company, Mr Kellock and Mr Michelmore, also Mr Wakeham (Dart Vale and Haldon), Mr Cockrem (Dartmoor), Mr Hurn (Mid Devon), Mr Luscombe (South Pool) and Mr Mildmay-White (Modbury). This Committee agreed that each hunt representative should return to their respective point-to-point and hunt committees in an endeavour to generate interest in subscribing to a fund comprising pledges from individual investors with a view to being able to bid at auction for the purchase of the racecourse, bungalow, ancillary buildings and land. Mr Wakeham was appointed to be the receiver of such pledges and it was thought that provided sufficient interest was shown then Totnes and Bridgetown Races Company would seriously consider some financial help towards the project if there was a shortfall of funds. The outcome of the exercise was that a very good response was forthcoming from members and supporters of the Dart Vale and Haldon Harriers but the other participating hunts were unable to generate any subscriptions at all, with some of their representatives speaking against the proposal as being a poor investment.

The Company felt that in the prevailing circumstances no further action could be taken regarding the sale and that the only hope for the continuation of racing at Buckfastleigh would be through the goodwill of the purchaser. It transpired that the new owners were to be Messrs N C Cooper & Sons who undertook an extensive enterprise of grain production which resulted in approximately half of the racing track being ploughed and sown. The Dart Vale and Haldon and South Pool hunts transferred their point-to-points to Bowden Pillars, Totnes, the Dartmoor and Modbury hunts raced at Kilworthy, Tavistock, before constructing a new course at Flete Park, Ermington, whilst the Mid Devon held their next meeting at Clyst Honiton. The situation at Buckfastleigh was to remain the same until 1999 when Messrs Cooper reinstated to grassland that part of the course which had been used for grain. Totnes and Bridgetown were to play no further role in the resumption of point to point racing at Buckfastleigh except through sponsorship of individual races, the Dart Vale & Haldon and South Pool Harriers being responsible for their own arrangements, the only hunts to return to the track.

The Company Dinner of 1980 boasted a plurality of guest speakers. It was held at The Holne Chase Hotel, Ashburton, with the guests enjoying the erudition and humour of Dr Colin MacVicar, Major Michael Howard, Lt. Cmdr. John Holdsworth, Mr John Tilling and Mr Denis Moore. The Company was represented by Mr J G Kellock, Mr R J Michelmore, Dr A McDowell Davies, Maj. R C Niles and Mr H J Harlow (Secretary). In addition to the speakers other guests were Dr I Barling, Mr A C Bulpin, Mr I S G Lang, Mr A J B Mildmay-White, Mr C Nekola, Cmdr. E W Sykes, Mr P J A Wakeham, Mr A R Todd, Mr C C Whitley and Mr R N Widdicombe.

In June 1982 the death occurred of Mr Joseph Grigg Kellock, a Director of the Company since 1933 and its Chairman since 1958, Mr Roger Michelmore being elected to fill the vacancy. In his end of year report, Mr Michelmore wrote, "Much of the progress of the Company is attributable to the wise guidance of the late Chairman and his name will long be remembered not only in Totnes but much further afield". The following year (1983) saw the appointment to the Company of Mr Peter J A Wakeham, to replace Mr Kellock with the addition of Mr Paul Clifford.

After an interval of three years, the next Company Dinner returned to the Holne Chase Hotel at which Directors, Mr R J Michelmore, Dr A McDowell Davies, Mr P Clifford, Maj. R C Niles, C.B.E., Mr P J A Wakeham and Mr H J Harlow (Secretary) were the hosts. Invited guests were Mr W. Beaumont, M.R.C.V.S., Lt. Cmdr. J A Holdsworth, C.V.O., O.B.E., Mr H D H Johnson (a Totnes solicitor who was a guest speaker), Mr I S G Lang, Mr R H Merton, Mr C Nekola, Cmdr. E W Sykes, D.S.C., Mr C C Whitley, Mr H J Widdicombe and Mr R N Widdicombe.

The Totnes & District Shows were and indeed are noted for their special attractions, entertainments and displays which are staged in the main ring during the afternoon. The Race Company was invited to contribute a recreational display of The Totnes and Bridgetown Races with a jumping course erected, with ponies and jockeys equipped with number cloths and sporting coloured silks together with a broadcast commentary on the racing and a 'potted history' of the races.

A request was received from Mr Bedward of the Totnes Community Archive, for the loan of the Company's old Minute books for research, as they were contemplating publishing a booklet on the racecourse and its activities. This was undertaken by Mrs Pauline Ferguson for a publication by Urban Earle in 1985. Mr David Thomas of the *Herald Express* also asked for information for an article which he proposed to write for the newspaper.

Director Dr Arthur McDowell Davies tendered his resignation from the Board on account of his leaving the district to reside at St. Mawes in Cornwall. He had served the Company for twenty-seven years since being elected in 1958.

Mr Richard Holdsworth whose father Capt. Frederick J C Holdsworth had been Chairman of the Company and a long-serving member, joined the Board in 1987, the same year that a Dinner was arranged to be held, after only a two year interval from its predecessor. This time the location had moved to the Furzeleigh Mill Country House Hotel at Buckfast, where Dr David Mills was the guest speaker. Dr Mills, a medical practitioner, was a former Master of the Britannia Beagles and a Joint Master of the Dartmoor Foxhounds. Company Directors Mr R J Michelmore, Mr P Clifford, Mr R A Holdsworth, Mr E J Holman, Mr P J A Wakeham, Maj. R C Niles and Mr H J Harlow (Secretary) were on hand to welcome their guests, Lord Courtenay, Mr W Goodman, Mr I S G Lang, Mr C Nekola, Mr J Vickers, Mr C C Whitley, Mr R N Widdicombe, Mr C R Willcocks and Mr K C Winchester.

At the end of 1988 Mr Jack Harlow retired from his position as the Company Secretary after a ten year period. In recognition of his commitment to the Board, the Chairman, Mr Michelmore, hosted a celebratory function at his home to mark the occasion and for the presentation of a gold watch. He was succeeded in office by Mr C C Curle.

1989 encompassed three movements registered within the Company. Mr Ted Holman stood down as Vice-Chairman and was replaced by Mr Paul Clifford. A new Director, Mr George Welch, was appointed, Mr Welch being the grandson of the previously mentioned Mr J G Kellock who was a well known Totnes solicitor and Chairman of the Devon & Cornwall Point-to-Point Association.

Yet another venue was chosen for the 1990 Company Dinner, the Elbow Room situated in the heart of Totnes. It was to be the only occasion that the venue was to be booked to host a Dinner due to the somewhat cramped conditions which restricted the number of invited guests. The guest speaker was Mr W Raleigh Gilbert, the well known course, ITV and Channel 4 commentator, who had commenced his career behind the microphone in this country at the West Country fixtures of Buckfastleigh and Newton Abbot, following his return from Kenya. Directors present were Mr R J Michelmore, Mr R A Holdsworth, Mr G K M Welch, Maj. R C Niles, Mr P J A Wakeham, Mr P Clifford and Mr C C Curle (Secretary) with guests Mr R N Widdicombe, Mr M Hancock, Mr F C Yeo, Maj. M Howard, Mr M D Rusden, Mr A E Sturges, Mr R J Vines, Mr K Winchester, Mr A J Goddard, Mr E A Darke, Mr C Nekola and Mr C R Willcocks.

Only two years had elapsed before diners were headed for the Glazebrook House Country Hotel for the renewal when the guest speaker was Mr Neil Wyatt, the Jockey Club Senior Inspector of Courses. For the Company, Mr R J Michelmore, Mr P Clifford, Mr R A Holdsworth, Mr E J Holman, Maj. R C Niles, Mr P J A Wakeham, Mr G K M Welch and Mr C C Curle (Secretary) were present together with guests, Mr E A Darke, Dr K M Fergusson, Maj. M

W Howard, Mr P C Kivell, Mr I S G Lang, Dr J MacPherson, Mr A Mildmay White, Mr C Nekola, Mr P J C Reade, Mr P D Rogers, Mr R Savery, His Grace the Duke of Somerset, Maj. L C Tar, Mr C M L Toll, Mr M Weir, Mr R Widdicombe, Mr C R Willcocks, Mr R J Hall and Mr F C Yeo.

The venue for the Company Dinner of 1995 was again the Glazebrook House Hotel, near South Brent, the guest speaker being Mr Michael Hancock, the Senior Jockey Club Judge, his family having been Jockey Club appointees in the role for over a century. The Company were represented by Mr R J Michelmore (Chairman), Mr E J Holman, Mr P Clifford, Mr P Wakeham, Mr G K M Welch, Mr R A Holdsworth and Mr C C Curle (Secretary). The guest list comprised Mr P Cooper, Mr B Crawford, Mr E A Darke, Mr P C Kivell, Mr I S G Lang, Mr P Masterson, Mr C Nekola, Miss J Newsome, Mr M D Rusden, Mr M Weir, Mr M B Ogle, Mrs A Ridgeway, Mr P D Rogers, Maj. L C Tar, Mr C M L Toll, Miss R A Tonks, Mrs M Trueman, Mr R N Widdicombe, Mr C R Willcocks and Mr F C Yeo.

The Company Secretary, Mr C C Curle, retired from office the following year after a tenure of seven years, the new appointment being Mrs Carol Godfrey. Mr Robert Savery became a Director in 1997 with Mr Paul Clifford being elected Vice-Chairman.

After a three year interval the next Company Dinner was again held at Glazebrook House Hotel at which the guest speaker was Mr Anthony Mildmay-White (nephew of the late Lord Mildmay of Flete), a prominent landowner and administrator in British racing. Directors in attendance were Mr R J Michelmore, Mr E J Holman, Mr R A Holdsworth, Mr M D Rusden, Mr R Savery, Mr P Wakeham, Mr G Welch and Mrs C Godfrey (Secretary). Others present were Mr S J Claisse, Mr Richard Cooper, Mr Roger Cooper, Mr C C Curle, Mr E A Darke, Mrs E N Duggleby, Mr R J Hall, Mr M E Hawkins, Mr A F Heath, Mr P C Kivell, Mr I S G Lang, Mr P G Masterson, Miss J M Michelmore, Mrs S Reynard, Mrs M A Ridgeway, Mr P D Rogers, Mr B W Soper, Mr C M L Toll, Mr M J Trickey, Mrs M Trueman, Mr M Weir, Mr R N Widdicombe and Mr C R Willcocks. The dinner was held to celebrate the re-opening of Buckfastleigh Racecourse and to mark the return of point-to-point racing to the course after an interval of twenty-one years. Totnes and Bridgetown were no longer players in arrangements between the landowners (Messrs N C Cooper & Sons) and the participating hunts, the Dart Vale and Haldon and South Pool Harriers which by this time had amalgamated. Under the regulations concerning Point-to-Point Racing where two hunts amalgamate then the combined committee may apply for two days racing in a season, which resulted in a February and a March meeting taking place.

Due to the shrewd and wise investment of their resources the Company were able to continue their usual racing sponsorship and to assist the local Pony Club with travelling expenses, an organisation that frequently provides the seed corn for the future equestrian star. In addition to the silver salver presented to the winner of a Hunter Steeplechase at Newton Abbot, a race whip is awarded to the winning rider. A perpetual silver trophy was donated to the Dartmoor and Modbury's two fixtures at Flete Park in 2000, for presentation to the leading novice rider at the course. At all race meetings where trophies were to be presented to winning owners in races sponsored by the Company a Director would be nominated to be on hand to 'do the honours'. This was to be the same year that the Company Secretary was to remarry and to appear in future references as Mrs Carol Richards.

2001 brought the resignation of Mr Paul Clifford as a Director due to leaving the area. Mr Michael Rusden filled the vacancy with Mr Peter Wakeham becoming Vice-Chairman. It was decided to extend the Company's sponsorship by providing the prizemoney for the three ridden hunter classes at Totnes & District Agricultural Show with ongoing support to the present day.

The Devon and Cornwall area's classic point-to-point race – the one race per area permitted to carry extra prizemoney – had since its inception been housed at the Tiverton Staghounds meeting. This hunt had indicated that it no longer wished to continue with its promotion, with the result that the race was transferred to the second Dart Vale and Haldon and South Pool Point to Point at Buckfastleigh. As this race was to be substituted for the Open race already sponsored by the Company, the Directors agreed to continue with their support and suggested that it be renamed "The West Country Champion 'Chase" which was accepted by the hunts.

Major Jeremy Kerr, a former racehorse owner and a Jockey Club Stewards Secretary was the guest speaker at the 2001 renewal Dinner. The Company was represented by Mr R J Michelmore, Mr P Wakeham, Mr E J Holman, Mr R A Holdsworth, Mr M D Rusden, Mr R Savery, Mr G Welch and Mrs C Richards (Secretary). On the guest list were: Mr E A Darke, Mr C De P Berry, Mr C J Down, Mr R F Eliot, Mr B Edmonds, Mrs A F Heath, Miss L Johnson, Mr I S G Lang, Miss J Michelmore, Mr P D Rogers, Mrs M Trueman, Mr R J Vines, Mrs P Watkins, Mr M Weir, Mr C R Willcocks and Mr F C Yeo, the event being held at Glazebrook House Hotel.

The passing of Mr Ivor Lang was recorded in 2003. He had a long association with the Race Company and had acted as their Clerk of the Course at Buckfastleigh for the point-to-point racing before being appointed in a similar capacity at Newton Abbot Racecourse. As an owner, he raced horses under both codes and was a local Inspector of Courses for Point-to-Points.

Mr Simon Claisse, the Chairman of the Point-to-Point Owners and Riders Association and the Clerk of the Course at Cheltenham, was invited to be guest speaker at the 2004 Company Dinner at Glazebrook. Directors in attendance were Mr R J Michelmore, Mr P Wakeham, Mr M D Rusden, Mr R Savery, Mr G Welch and Mr R A Holdsworth whilst the guests were Mr B

Crawford, Mr E A Darke, Mr C De P Berry, Mr J Frost, Mr A Mildmay-White, Mr I A Pearse, Mr P D Rogers, Mr B W Soper, Mrs M Trueman, Maj. Gen. N Vaux, Mrs P Watkins, Mr M Weir, Mr I Widdicombe and Mr C R Willcocks.

By 2006 the permitted prizemoney for the West Country Champion 'Chase at the Dart Vale and Haldon and South Pool Harriers Point-to-Point had been increased to a total of £1,000 by special dispensation from the Jockey Club and the British Horseracing Board and to be recognised as one of the six premier point-to-point races in the country. This accolade was achieved through the campaigning of Mr Peter Wakeham and his successors, Mr Peter Kivell and Mr Frank Yeo, as Chairmen of the Devon and Cornwall Point to Point Association, in their efforts to further upgrade the race. Totnes and Bridgetown Races Company were pleased to continue their sponsorship, with the winning owner's prizemoney of £700 being the highest amount awarded in the Point-to-Point calendar. The promoting hunts played their part by including a thumb sketch of the owners' colours in the racecard for their feature race.

The Company were able to purchase a second silver cup engraved 'Totnes Races 1794, John Hayles Sheckle, Esq. (presumably the donor), won by Sportsman, Property of Thomas Peeke, Esq.' Unlike the other cup in the Company's possession this trophy has a tap attachment as may be seen from the photograph. It is thought that the winning owner, Mr Peeke, was a member of the family currently residing in the Washbourne area between Harbertonford and Halwell and previously at Painsford, Ashprington. The purchase of this cup was somewhat fortuitous as a silver dealer in Surrey had telephoned the administrator of Totnes Museum to inform him that he had it in his possession, at the same time that the Chairman of the Races Company was in his presence. The Museum was to hold an exhibition featuring Totnes Races in 2008 for which both cups with other memorabilia were loaned by the Directors. It is of interest to learn that another early Totnes silver cup (1789) is on display at Greenway house, Galmpton, near Brixham. It was formerly the property of the author, Agatha Christie, before being inherited by her daughter, Mrs Rosalind Hicks, following whose death it became part of the Christie artefacts now managed by the National Trust. A photograph of the trophy is to be found in this book.

2007 brought the resignation of the Company Secretary, Mrs Richards, the position being filled by Mrs Moira Aylett. This year saw arrangements being made for the next Dinner and a change of venue, the event being transferred to the Ilsington Country House Hotel, Bovey Tracey. The invited speaker was Mr Derek Lever, a racecourse announcer and Jockey Club Judge. It is Company policy to vary its guest list to enable inclusion of additional persons who have significantly contributed to the racing scene. This year the guests included two National Champion amateur riders: Miss Polly Gundry –

a seven times Point-to-Point Champion at the time of writing – and Mr Leslie Jefford, the National Champion of 2000 under the same code, also the amateur champion of flat racing in the same year. Making up the complement for the guests were Mr G T Chambers, Mr B Crawford, Mr E A Darke, Mr J Greatrex, Mr R J Hall, Miss L Johnson, Mrs D Michelmore, Miss J M Michelmore, Mr R H G Michelmore, Mr A J B Mildmay-White, Mr I A Pearse, Mrs S Reynard, Mr P D Rogers, Mr B W Soper, Mr M Treneer, Mrs M Trueman, Mr C R Willcocks and Mr F C Yeo. The Company was represented by Mr R J Michelmore, Mr P Wakeham, Mr W J Goodman, Mr R A Holdsworth, Mr M D Rusden, Mr R Savery, Mr G Welch and the Secretary, Mrs M Aylett.

After a period of twenty-six years in office, Mr Roger Michelmore indicated that he did not wish to seek nomination for the position as Chairman of the Company for the ensuing year, Mr Peter Wakeham being elected to fill the vacancy. Mr Michelmore accepted the role as Vice-Chairman. The advent of the 2008-09 Point-to-Point season brought the further upgrading of the West Country Champion Steeplechase at Buckfastleigh to become included as a race in the Point-to-Point 'Order of Excellence'. The idea of this Order is to find the best point-to-pointer of the season, by putting together a series of races, one in each area of the country, which attracts points. The horse winning the greatest number of points in total will acquire a trophy and memento. The six 'classic' races, of which the West Country Champion 'Chase is one, will carry an additional number of points to other qualifying races, with twelve points going to the winner and with extra prizemoney to that advertised (£700 in the Company's race) to the extent of £30 per point. The successful owner of the winner 'Rockwithacaveman', Mr R J Pike, thereby received an extra £360 on the day. Director Mr Richard Holdsworth who had served the Company since his appointment in 1987 resigned in 2008. During his tenure he had compiled the album of Totnes Races memorabilia, of newspaper reports, both original and photocopies, together with racecards and photographs which had been acquired over a number of years and which I have found extremely useful in producing this book. Two new appointments to the Board were forthcoming in 2009: Mrs Mary Trueman who has the distinction of being the first lady Director in the history of the Company and Mr Anthony Mildmay-White.

It was decided that with the amount of material that had been accumulated over the years by the Company and with the Holdsworth album which contained information which had been retained by Alfred Hingston, a former Director, as a nucleus for consultation, that a history of the Races, racecourse and Company should be compiled in a book, to which task I have set my hand.

2009. Mr W J Goodman (left) with Mr J F Symes, owner of Whizzaar and rider Mr R Woollacott following presentation of trophies for the Men's Open Race at South Pool Point-to-Point, Buckfastleigh
Photo courtesy of Total Leigh

2008. Mrs M Trueman, now a Director of the Company, having received a silver salver from Mr M D Rusden, following the success of DeLuain Gorm in the Totnes Novice Hunter Steeplechase, Newton Abbot with rider Mr G Gallagher

Photo courtesy of Fiona Crawford

2008. Mr W J Goodman with Mr and Mrs R Hand, owners of Dante's Back and rider Mr D Edwards, winners of the Men's Open Race at South Pool Point-to-Point, Buckfastleigh
Photo courtesy of Hamish Mitchell

2009. Mr R J Michelmore presenting trophies to Mr R J Pike, owner of Rockwithacaveman, successful in the Westcountry Champion Steeplechase, Dart Vale & Haldon Point-to-Point at Buckfastleigh with rider Miss P Gundry,

Photo courtesy of Turfpix

2009. Mr P J A Wakeham presenting a silver salver to Mr I Prichard, owner of Alroyal, winner of the Totnes Novice Hunter Steeplechase, Newton Abbot

Photo courtesy of Fiona Crawford

Company Dinner guests at The Elbow Room, Totnes, 1990

2009 Company Dinner; Ilsington Country House Hotel

Agatha Christie Silver Cup dated 1789, inscribed Richard Strode Esq.,
Steward. Now on display at Greenway House, Galmpton

First and second day Admission Tickets to Grandstand 1900; also two Starter/Auctioneer badges 1926

TOTNES RACES

Wednesday and Thursday,
SEPT. 6TH & 7TH, 1939

UNDER NATIONAL HUNT RULES.   FOLLOWING THE DEVON AND EXETER MEETING.

Patrons. THE DUKE OF SOMERSET, LORD MAMHEAD; THE LORD MILDMAY OF FLETE; Sir ALFRED GOODSON, Bart.; Major Sir SAMUEL E. HARVEY; Commdr. C. H. DAVEY, R.N., O.B.E., M.F.H.; G. H. TURNER, Esq.

Directors. Capt. F. J. C. HOLDSWORTH (Chairman), Lt.-Col. F. K. WINDEATT; Mr. A. HINGSTON; Mr. W. R. HOLMAN; Capt. H. B. KAUNTZE; Mr. J. G. KELLOCK; Mr. G. F. B. MARKS; and Major W. G. LOVEYS.

Stewards. Capt. R. D. WORRALL, M.C. H. F. BRUNSKILL, Esq. Major F. H. B. PASSY. J. G. KELLOCK, Esq.

Officials. Mr. R. TURNER, Handicapper; Mr. J. WAKEHAM, Marley, South Brent, Hon. Starter & Auctioneer; Mr. A. E. HANCOCK, Judge; Mr. H. L. CROCKWELL, Clerk of the Scales; Dr. STANLEY C. JELLICOE, Surgeon; Capt. H. B. KAUNTZE, M.R.C.V.S., Veterinary Surgeon; Mr. J. MASON, 59, Fore Street, Totnes, Secretary; Lt.-Col. F. K. WINDEATT, Elmfield, Totnes, Stakeholder; Mr. T. H. WILTON PYE, Broad Street Chambers, 32, Broad Street, Worcester, Clerk of the Course.

STAKES £865

Programmes and further particulars to be obtained from Mr. J. MASON, 59, Fore Street, Totnes, Secretary; or Mr. T. H. WILTON PYE, Broad Street Chambers, 32, Broad Street, Worcester, Clerk of the Course.

FIRST DAY:
SIX RACES value £435
1st Race starts 3 p.m.

SECOND DAY:
SIX RACES value £430
1st Race starts 2-30 p.m.

THE TOTALISATOR
will be in operation, staffed and operated by the Racecourse Betting Control Board.

Win and Place Tickets will be available at 2/- & 10/-
The Totalisator will pay out on three places when there are seven or more horses declared to start, and two places when there are five or six horses declared to start. If less than five horses are declared to start, there will be no Place Betting.

FORECAST POOL. In any Race where there is no Place Betting & there are only three or four horses declared to start, a Forecast Pool (2/- and 10/- Tickets) will be operated. A correct forecast is one which nominates the first and second horses in their correct order in any particular race.

DAILY DOUBLE. Daily Double Tickets can be purchased from the Totalisator, Price 10/-. The selected Races for the Double Event are Races Three and Five.

PRICES OF ADMISSION EACH DAY:
To COURSE, 2/- (including Tax). To STAND AND PADDOCK (Course Entrance), 10/- (including tax). To COURSE, STAND AND PADDOCK (Back of Stand Entrance), 12/- (including Tax). MOTOR CARS going on the Course, 10/- Occupants 2/- in addition (including Tax). CARS carrying more than six persons, 20/-. Occupants 2/-. in addition (including Tax). BOOKMAKERS will be charged as follows for their Pitches, in addition to the ordinary Admission Charge : Stand and Paddock Enclosure, 30/-; Course, 6/-.

For the convenience of persons attending the Races, who do not wish to drive on the Race Course, arrangements have been made with the Totnes Town Council to have the use of part of the TOTNES BOROUGH PARK for the purpose of PARKING CARS on the two days of Racing, at the following charges :—Chars-a-banc, 3/6 each per day; Motor Cars and Motor Horse Boxes, 2/6 each per day; Motor Cycles, 1/6 each per day.

SOLE CATERING RIGHTS in the hands of Mr. E. H. GIFFORD, East Gate Inn, TOTNES.
LUNCHEONS & TEAS will be supplied in the GRAND STAND ENCLOSURE and on the COURSE at MODERATE PRICES.

The Public will be admitted to the Course at 12 o'clock each day. No Charabancs, Shows, Shooting Galleries, Living Vans, Hot Chip Potato Vans, Glass Ball or Bottle Shooting, etc., will be allowed within the circle of the Race Course. J. MASON, Sec., 59, Fore St., Totnes.

MORTIMER BROS., PRINTERS AND PUBLISHERS, TOTNES.

Poster of abandoned fixture 1939

IN MEMORIAM

As a postscript, it may be considered appropriate that a final assessment and comment on Totnes Races should be the gift of other scribes.

In his booklet of 1985 Urban Earle with the assistance of his researcher, Mrs Pauline Ferguson, writes, "Broadmarsh, the site of the racecourse now houses an industrial estate but evidence of its former use survives in the remnants of the grandstand and outbuildings such as the stables and the platform on which the number board was raised." His conclusion was that the great success of Totnes and Bridgetown Races meeting was attributable to a variety of factors. That it was for so long a free course undoubtedly did much to encourage its popularity. A correspondent for the *Totnes Times* wrote in 1881 that, "The Plymouth Races seem to be dying out, if one is to judge by the small attendance at them year after year." He attributed this in part to the fact that an entrance fee to the course was payable. At Totnes, the railway station being adjacent to the course facilitated the transport of both spectators and horses. At Exeter there was a considerable distance between the railway station and the racecourse which was situated at Haldon.

The geography of the region was also to Totnes' advantage, Plymouth and Exeter being equidistant and Dartmouth being well served with the river steamer traffic. Many spectators used the railway to come from South Brent, Newton Abbot, Torquay, Dawlish and Paignton. The timing of the meeting at the beginning of September meant that the harvest was in (or almost in) and the agricultural workers free to attend. If the meeting was held any later, there was always the possibility that the weather could ruin it, sometimes conflicts with the dates of other race meetings or regattas necessitated the meeting being held later and if the weather held out, usually large attendances ensued.

Ironically it was largely the very unsuitability of Totnes for racing which was responsible for its success. The inclusion of two crossings of the Dart and a straight of only 300 yards may have been the cause of much amusement for those who chose to compare the meeting to those at Newmarket and other more sophisticated courses, but it provided a spectacle which many found irresistible.

Urban Earle continued, "Walking on Broadmarsh today, it is difficult to imagine that at one time tens of thousands of spectators and hundreds of carriages and booths, filled this small oval of land. If one climbs on to the old grandstand (now a goods store) one can however still enjoy the same view of the hills over which the legendary steeplechases were once run."

These sentiments were mirrored by Chris Pitt in his excellent publication, *A Long Time Gone*, adding that, "its heritage is recalled only by a road sign to 'The Paddock Industrial Units'. The grandstand and stable blocks were there until a few years ago, being used as storage sheds but have now been demolished and replaced by town houses. The only sport there today is that provided by Totnes Rugby Club." He went on to say, "When I visited Broadmarsh in December 1993, I found it hard to conceive that tens of thousands of cheering spectators once filled this small oval of land. The siding from Totnes station, located directly behind the grandstand has been dismantled though the path to the racecourse is still there, as is what looks to have once been a box for selling racecards at the entrance to the track." Chris Pitt concludes, "The course is gone though not forgotten. For through the auspices of Totnes and Bridgetown Races Company Ltd the memory of racing at Broadmarsh lives on."

That memory and the continuation of the Company remain in the hands of the Board of Directors who are responsible for its well being and who are listed below:

Mr Peter J A Wakeham (Chairman)

Mr Roger J Michelmore (Vice-Chairman)
Auctioneer, estate and land agent; former Magistrate; member of Dartmoor Commoners' Council; Director of the Company since 1958, Chairman for twenty-six years.

Mr Edward J Holman
Former Director of Messrs W R Holman & Son, Seed Merchants; succeeded his father on the Board in 1958; a racecourse Jockey Club Judge now retired; the only Director to have attended a Totnes and Bridgetown race meeting.

Mr George K M Welch
Landowner and farmer; Director of Newton Abbot Races Ltd.; a licensed racecourse Steward under Jockey Club Rules and grandson of former Chairman, Mr J G Kellock; Director since 1989.

Mr Michael D Rusden
Landowner and farmer; former licensed racecourse Steward under Jockey Club Rules; successful racehorse owner, National Hunt and point-to-points; appointed Director in 2001.

Mr Robert Savery
Landowner and farmer; member of Dartmoor Commoners' Council; Patron of the Living of St. Mary's Church, Rattery; appointed as Director in 1996.

Mr W John Goodman
Landowner and farmer; Point-to-Point Steward; his father was a Joint Master

of the Dartmoor Hunt; a Director since 2007.

Mr Anthony J B Mildmay-White
Landowner and member of the Jockey Club with service on several of its committees; a licensed racecourse Steward under Jockey Club Rules; former Chairman of Newton Abbot Races Ltd. and High Sheriff of Devon; appointed a Director in 2009; his grandfather Mr F B Mildmay was a Steward at Totnes and he is the nephew of the late Lord Mildmay of Flete.

Mrs Mary Trueman
Landowner and farmer; member of the Coulton family associated with Buckfastleigh Races for over seventy years at which her father was Clerk of the Course; former Chairman and President of Totnes Show and former Chairman of the Modbury Harriers; a successful racehorse owner; appointed to the Board in 2009.

So what was the magic formula that drew people to the Totnes and Bridgetown Races? Perhaps one reason was given by the ninety-four year old lady from Broadhempston in 1860 who having walked the six miles each way to attend the races said, "It makes me feel quite young again".

1996: Senior Jockey Club Judge Mr Michael Hancock presenting a painting to Mr Ted Holman upon his retirement as a Licensed Racecourse Judge

BIBLIOGRAPHY

Kingsbridge and Salcombe R. Southwood
A Race Apart Reg Green
The South Devon Hunt Edward J. F. Tozer
A Long Time Gone Chris Pitt
Cope's Racegoers Encyclopaedia Alfred Cope
Ras Prince Monolulu Simon H. White
Anthony Mildmay Roger Mortimer
Mercy Rimell, Reflections on Racing Ivor Herbert
Lester Dick Francis
Racing Calendars
Newspapers: *The Western Morning News*
　　　　　　The Totnes Times
　　　　　　The South Devon Journal
Totnes and Bridgetown Urban Earle